A North American Indian brave would leave a single scalp lock on an otherwise shaven head so that a conquering enemy could seize it to tear off the scalp. A gruesome challenge!

1

The famous polar explorer Roald Amundsen became Norway's first civilian air pilot in 1914. A quicker way to travel than skis or sledge!

The first gallery in a theatre or opera house is called the dress circle.

A North American Indian brave would leave a single scalp-lock on an otherwise shaven head so that a conquering enemy could seize it to tear off the scalp. A gruesome challenge!

The longest monosyllables in the English language are 'screeched' and 'stretched'.

The first in a long line of royal corgis was Dooky, bought in 1933 by the Duke of York (later George VI), when his eldest daughter, now Queen Elizabeth II, was about seven years old.

Apsley House, now a museum but once the city residence of the great Duke of Wellington (1769–1852), was known simply and with deep affection as No 1, London.

By 1811 the population of London had topped the 1 million mark, making it the largest city in the world.

Many one-eyed people have reached the height of success in their chosen professions, witness the inventor Guglielmo Marconi, film director John Ford, actor Rex Harrison and politician Moshe Dayan.

To the Romans the first days of the months were the *calends* – hence the word calendar.

The only large mammal species discovered this century is the okapi, first spotted in the Congo, Africa, in 1901. It is related to the giraffe, but is shorter in the legs and neck.

2

A young cow is called a heifer until the birth of her second calf.

Binary is a mathematical system used in computers, etc., in which numbers are expressed by using only two digits – 1 and 0 – represented by an on/off electrical switch.

There are only two tailless breeds of cats: the Manx cat and the Japanese bobtail, a very rare species found in parts of Japan.

The Anglo-French supersonic air liner Concorde was designed to travel at Mach 2 (up to 1,400 mph; 2,253 kph) – twice the speed of sound!

Twice an hour, at a precisely determined interval, all ships' transmitters are silenced so that wireless operators will be able to hear even the faintest 'mayday' distress call.

By English law a person making a will must have two witnesses to all his signatures.

In the equine world a nursery is a race for two-year-old horses.

Mount St Helens, Washington, has been much in the news since 1980, when the first of several recent eruptions occurred. Together with Lassen Peak, California, last active in 1917, they represent the only two active volcanoes on mainland USA.

Semi, demi and hemi are prefixes meaning half or divided into two.

Jean-Paul Marat, an infamous leader of the French Revolution, needed only two hours of sleep a night. He was caught napping when Charlotte Corday stabbed him to death in his bath in July 1793.

3

Wisdom teeth, the popular name for the third molar in each jaw, normally appear between the ages of seventeen and twenty-five.

Tony Jacklin and Sandy Lyle have had their moments of golfing glory, but England's best ever player was probably Henry Cotton, who won the British Open in 1934, 1937 and 1948.

The only horse ever to win the Grand National steeplechase at Aintree three times was the remarkable Red Rum in 1973, 1974 and 1977.

A monk's girdle has three knots to signify the vows of poverty, chastity and obedience.

A three-year-old salmon is called a mort.

Since AD 1200 banns – a declaration of intent – have been read out at morning service in Christian churches on three successive Sundays to announce a forthcoming marriage.

The only three British Prime Ministers never to live at 10 Downing Street, London, were Viscount Melbourne, Sir Robert Peel and the Marquess of Salisbury.

Only three British women have won the Ladies Singles Championship at Wimbledon since World War II. They are Angela Mortimer (1961), Ann Jones (1969) and Virginia Wade (1977).

A one-year-old baby is about three times its weight at birth.

A family-size igloo is approximately 3 m (10 ft) wide.

4

With an average of 911 people to a square mile (1·6 sq km), England is four times as crowded as China!

The four most frequently recorded song titles are 'Yesterday', 'Stardust', 'St Louis Blues' and 'Tie a Yellow Ribbon'.

A biretta is a four-cornered head covering worn by Roman Catholic priests.

The four biggest planets – Saturn, Uranus, Neptune and Jupiter – are just gas!

Every country in North and South America declared war on Germany in World War II, but only four – Brazil, Canada, Mexico and the USA – actually provided fighting forces.

'I'm dreaming of a white Christmas . . .' Snow has fallen in London on Christmas Day (which is just four days into winter) on only four occasions this century: 1927, 1938, 1970 and 1981.

The most potent bomber planes of World War II were Avro Lancasters, used in massive night attacks on Germany. Of 7,000 built, only four remain today.

Four men in every ten are colour-blind.

Only four people are empowered to issue 'By Appointment', the royal seal of approval for food or goods tested over a period of time. They are the Queen, the Duke of Edinburgh, the Queen Mother and the Prince of Wales.

The main runway at Schiphol Airport in Amsterdam, Holland, is 4 m (13 ft) below sea level.

5

A cat can be in season up to five times a year, and will have an average litter of five kittens. It is not surprising therefore that there are 5 million cats in the UK.

These days most schoolchildren are taught how to construct the five regular solids: the tetrahedron, hexahedron, octahedron, dodecahedron and icosahedron. Crystals of common salt are hexahedral, while those of diamonds are octahedral.

The five wits are said to be common sense, imagination, fantasy, estimation and memory. Who would disagree?

Mary Quant, the young London designer who introduced British girls to the mini-skirt, uses a five-petalled daisy as her trademark.

Limericks are five-line nonsense verses in which the first, second and last lines all rhyme, while the shorter third and fourth lines have a different rhyme.

Bethlehem, the birthplace of Jesus, is only 5 miles (8 km) south of Jerusalem, where he spent the last week before his crucifixion. Both places are now under Israeli administration.

Pental, lustrum and quinquennium are all words meaning a period of five years.

Since its official opening on 19 March 1932 as the world's largest bridge, Sydney Harbour Bridge in Australia has been painted only five times.

Between 1929 and 1940 the Soviet Union experimented with a five day week.

A lion's roar can be heard over a distance of 5 miles (8 km).

6

There are six common patterns for fingertip skin ridges: double loop, tented loop, radial loop, arch, whorl and ulnar loop. No two persons, however, not even identical twins, have exactly the same fingerprints.

Hens start to lay eggs when they are six months old.

German is spoken in six European countries: Austria, East Germany, West Germany, Liechtenstein, Luxembourg and Switzerland.

Rats and mice like few things better than a tasty diet of paper. Aware of this, the British Museum in London keeps six cats (Susie, Tiger, Daisy, Bertie, Victoria and Albert), which are fed on only six days of the week – on Sunday they must earn their keep!

Six notable actors have portrayed Dr Who in the popular BBC television serial since 1963 – William Hartnell, Patrick Troughton, Jon Pertwee, Tom Baker, Peter Davison and Colin Baker.

To gain a licence, a London taxi-driver must prove to a selection board that he has a detailed knowledge of all the streets and important buildings within 6 miles (9·6 km) of Charing Cross.

A team of fifty-five doctors and nurses was needed to safely deliver Britain's first ever surviving sextuplets – the Walton girls – at Liverpool on 18 November 1983.

Charles I (1601–49) was six before he could speak or walk.

Most countries of the world find the growth in population a problem. However, there are six nations, – all in Europe – who have shrinking populations: Austria, Denmark, East Germany, West Germany, Hungary and Sweden.

Light travels through air six times as fast as it does through water.

7

Whitsun is the seventh Sunday after Easter day.

The seven primary odours are: camphoraceous, ethereal, floral, musky, peppermint, pungent and putrid. All smells – pleasant or otherwise – are complexes of these basic scents.

The largest present ever accepted by the Queen was a 7·1 tonne (7 ton) elephant called Jumbo, now resident in Whipsnade Zoo, which was given to her during the 1977 Silver Jubilee Celebrations.

Seat No C7 in the reading room of the British Museum in London has a special significance. It was there that the German philosopher Karl Marx (1818–83) wrote *Das Kapital*, germane to the spread of communism.

Henry Foster, a Malvern priest, had seven sons, all of whom played cricket for Worcestershire between 1899 and 1934.

One of Henry VIII's greatest interests was hunting. When he wished to call his dogs, he would give a strong blast on a whistle studded with seven diamonds.

The Plough is a group of seven large, bright stars which appear to form the outline of a wagon or wheelbarrow. It is also known as the Great Bear and Charles's Wain.

Seven different languages are spoken in Yugoslavia.

The Australian state of Queensland is seven times the size of the UK.

Ostriches can cover 7·6 m (25 ft) at a single stride. Only a handful of long-jumpers have ever leapt this distance.

8

Dr Samuel Johnson took eight years to complete his famous dictionary, begun in 1747.

At 12·34 on 5 June 1978, the time and date could be reduced to 12345678.

Only eight colours were used in the Bayeux Tapestry.

George Washington (1732–99), the first US president, remained in office for eight years from 1789–97. Interestingly he never lived in the American capital named after him.

Eight Britons have been deemed worthy of a state funeral paid for by the government. They were the Earl of Chatham, his son William Pitt, Viscount Nelson, the Duke of Wellington, Mr Gladstone, Earl Roberts, Viscount Alanbrooke and Sir Winston Churchill.

America has eight women golf millionaires.

Zambia and the Congo are each surrounded by eight other nations.

Monks attend eight church services during the course of a day.

In the seventeenth century the popularity of the new beverage tea caused a dramatic fall in the sale of wine in London's taverns. So much so that Charles II had to impose a duty of 8d a gallon on tea to make up for declining revenue!

In Victorian times it was the ambition of mountaineers to scale the 4,500 m (14,763 ft) high Matterhorn, the most striking of Alpine peaks. The first to do so, but only at his eighth attempt, was a twenty-five-year-old Englishman, Edward Whymper, on 14 July 1865.

9

Morocco (Africa) and Spain (Europe) are only 9 miles (14 km) apart across the Strait of Gibraltar, the entrance to the Mediterranean Sea.

There are only nine paintings in existence by the Florentine genius, Leonardo da Vinci (1452–1519).

Much of what we know about the early reign of Charles II and of events like the Great Fire and the Great Plague of London is culled from the diary of Samuel Pepys (1633–1703), an official in the Admiralty, who wrote in precise detail about the nine years from 1 January 1660, to 31 May 1669. He discontinued writing when his wife died and his eyesight began to fail him.

The Red Arrows, the RAF aerobatic display team formed in 1964, have added spectacle to shows throughout the UK and abroad. Since 1980 the team has consisted of nine Hawk aircraft, flying at speeds of about 350 mph (563 kph).

The General Strike of 1926, which brought Britain to a halt, was born out of a miners' dispute with the coal owners. It lasted for nine days from 4 May to 13 May.

Nine per cent of a bottle of Coca-Cola is sugar.

Mary Tudor ('Bloody Mary'), who as Queen of England between 1553 and 1558 was responsible for 383 non-Catholics being burnt at the stake, was deeply religious and attended Mass nine times a day.

Nylon stockings are usually 9-denier – about five times as thin as a human hair.

John Lowe will never forget 13 October 1984, when he became the first person in competition to make a perfect nine throw in a 501-up game of darts. For the record, he made two maximum 180s, a treble 17, a treble 18 and a double 18. Some throwing!

England's smallest bird, the goldcrest, is 9 cm (3½ in) in length.

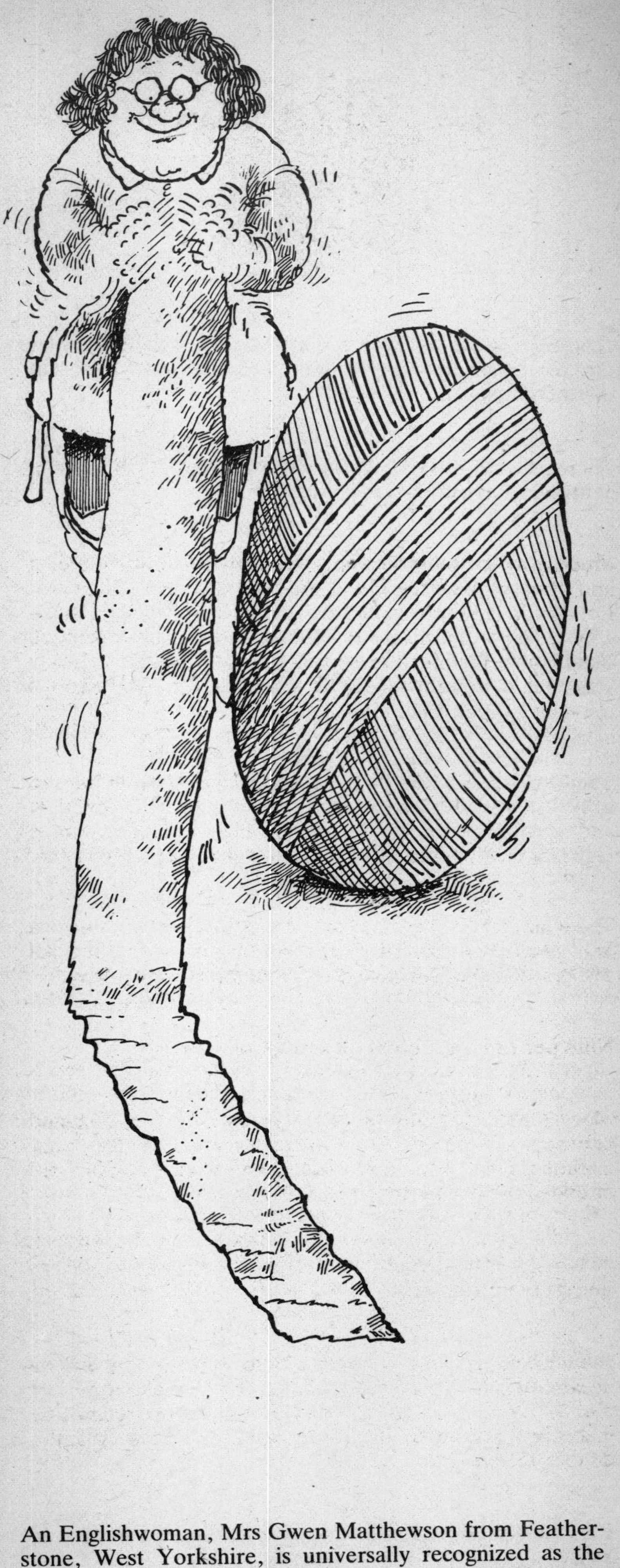

An Englishwoman, Mrs Gwen Matthewson from Featherstone, West Yorkshire, is universally recognized as the world's fastest knitter at 111 stitches a minute. She once knitted a 10 m (34 ft) long scarf in ninety minutes on the David Frost television show *The Record Breakers*.

10

The Decalogue is another word for the Ten Commandments, which are duplicated in Exodus xx, 1–17 and Deuteronomy v, 6–21 in the Old Testament.

There are ten countries in Africa where men are not expected to reach the age of forty!

Every year 10 million people are arrested in the USA.

A ten-gallon hat, as worn by Texans, actually holds only 3·4 litres (6 pt).

The word 'ace' – denoting excellence – was used originally by the French during World War I to honour a pilot who had destroyed a minimum of ten German aircraft.

The prefix 'deca' means ten-fold, while 'deci' means one-tenth.

All the New York skyscrapers are tightly packed together within an area of 10 sq miles (25·9 sq km) on the lower half of Manhattan Island, between the Hudson and East rivers.

It cost Prince Philip of Greece the standard £10 fee to become a naturalized British subject, plain Philip Mountbatten, in 1947.

An Englishwoman, Mrs Gwen Matthewson from Featherstone, West Yorkshire, is universally recognized as the world's fastest knitter at 111 stitches a minute. She once knitted a 10 m (34 ft) long scarf in ninety minutes on the David Frost television show *The Record Breakers*.

Bananas grow in areas where the temperature never falls below 10°C (50°F).

11

The smell of diesel fumes can be most offensive today, but imagine what it was like in London a hundred years ago when there were 11,000 horse drawn cabs in the city!

OPEC is a cartel of eleven member countries which control the world price of that essential commodity, oil. They are Ecuador, Venezuela, Algeria, Libya, Nigeria, Gabon, Iraq, Iran, Kuwait, Saudi Arabia and Qatar.

Franklin D. Roosevelt (1882–1945), the thirty-second US president, was related to five others by blood and a further six by marriage.

The person who looks after Britain's money is the Chancellor of the Exchequer. His official London residence is 11 Downing Street, next door to you know who!

At present only 11 per cent of the world's surface is cultivated.

William Shakespeare is known to have spelt his surname eleven different ways.

Eleven of the original twelve apostles came from Galilee, the exception being the treacherous Judas Iscariot, who hailed from Kerioth, a village in Judea.

Dutch elm disease, caused by a beetle burrowing beneath the bark, has destroyed 11 million trees in England during the last eleven years.

World War I ended officially at the eleventh hour of the eleventh day of the eleventh month of 1918, following the signing of an Armistice in a railway coach in the forest of Compiègne, outside Paris.

By the time Britain and its American colonies adopted the Gregorian calendar in 1752, the old Julian calendar was eleven days out of date. The solution was to drop all dates between 3 September and 13 September of that year.

12

Pluto, the planet farthest away from the sun, is about twelve times as dense as Earth. There the average human being would weigh 323 kg (51 st)!

The Battle of Britain lasted for twelve weeks from 10 July to 31 October 1940: 1,733 German aircraft were destroyed for the loss of 915 British planes, and the threat of enemy invasion vanished.

'The Glorious Twelfth', 12 August, is the official start of the grouse shooting season, which lasts for seventeen weeks. Incidentally, it is illegal to shoot these game birds on a Sunday.

The American singer Frank Sinatra gives twelve charity concerts every year.

Ruth Lawrence became the youngest-ever student at Oxford University when in 1984, at the age of twelve, she became a first-year undergraduate at St Hugh's College, reading mathematics.

When she was only twelve, the future Elizabeth I was imprisoned in the Tower of London at the behest of her older half-sister Queen Mary Tudor.

The oriental zodiac or calendar is based on a twelve year cycle. The first year is the Year of the Rat, then come the Year of the Ox,Tiger, Hare, Dragon, Snake, Horse, Ram, Monkey, Cockerel, Dog and Pig. As it is based on the phases of the moon, the date of the Chinese New Year varies, though it is always between 20 January and 20 February.

Sir Galahad was said to be the bravest and purest of King Arthur's twelve Knights of the Round Table. According to legend it was he who, after many exciting adventures, finally found in a cave the Holy Grail, the sacred cup Jesus had used at the Last Supper.

During the twelve years (1603–15) he spent imprisoned in the Tower of London, Sir Walter Raleigh wrote his famous *History of the World.*

In Paris, twelve avenues converge at L'Étoile, where the Arc de Triomphe stands.

13

An opossum gives birth to an average litter of thirteen young after only thirteen days.

China and the USSR each have frontiers with thirteen other countries.

The world's first skyscraper, the thirteen storey Tacoma Building, was erected in Chicago, USA, in 1889.

Before blended sherry is finally bottled, thirteen egg whites are whisked well into a little sherry and then added to each cask in order that unwanted particles will adhere and be dragged to the bottom, so ensuring perfect clarity.

There are thirteen legal coins and notes in US currency.

Caterpillars have thirteen segments to their bodies.

Queen Cleopatra of Egypt was fluent in thirteen languages.

In the seventeenth century women in the USA produced an average of thirteen children each!

Gioacchino Rossini (1792–1868) wrote his comic masterpiece *The Barber of Seville* in just thirteen days. It has remained one of the most popular of operas since its first performance at Rome in February 1816.

In the UK a child of thirteen can legally take a part-time job as long as it is light work (a paper round, for example), and involves him or her for no longer than two hours on a weekday or for one hour on a Sunday.

14

The Queen Mother celebrated her fourteenth birthday on 4 August 1914, the day Great Britain declared war on Germany.

A measles rash lasts for fourteen days.

A post-mortem on Elvis Presley (1935–77) revealed the presence of fourteen different drugs in his bloodstream.

In 1981 Andrea Jaeger of the USA became the youngest-ever tennis player of either sex to be seeded at Wimbledon. She was only fourteen years old.

An amazing 845 languages and dialects are spoken in India, but the National Constitution recognizes only fourteen with Hindi as the most important.

An estimated 14 million African slaves were shipped to North and South America during the seventeenth and eighteenth centuries. The 14th Amendment of the US Constitution, proclaimed on 28 July 1868, gave all former slaves full rights as citizens.

In the time of Christ the warm waters of the Sea of Galilee contained fourteen kinds of fish, including carp, perch, bream and the small 'St Peter's fish'. Jewish law forbids the eating of such scaleless fish as eels and catfish.

A golfer is allowed to use up to fourteen clubs.

In 1896 the Locomotives Act repealed the 'red flag' restriction and allowed a maximum speed of 14 mph (22·5 kph) on British roads.

The celebrated seventeenth-century portrait painter Sir Godfrey Kneller was in such demand that he would see as many as fourteen sitters a day. He made quick crayon sketches and would paint them in oil later.

15

A free range hen – so rare these days – regularly lays a clutch of up to fifteen eggs.

Fifteen English Kings and Queens Regnant have been buried at Westminster Abbey.

Only fifteen people live on Lundy Island, 23 miles (37 km) out in the Bristol Channel from Ilfracombe. They are vastly out-numbered by puffins!

A person who smokes twenty cigarettes a day is fifteen times more likely to contract lung cancer than a non-smoker.

There are fifteen rail termini in London.

Only fifteen teams competed in the first FA Cup Competition in 1872. A hundred years later 480 sides were involved.

Colman's, a Norwich firm founded in 1814, produce fifteen types of mustard from locally grown seed.

John Tyler, the tenth US president (1841–45), had fifteen children, eight by his first wife and seven by his second, which constitutes a record for any holder of that office.

The mad but brilliant Dutch artist Vincent van Gogh (1853–90) feverishly completed 200 paintings in the last fifteen months of his tragic life.

Adult hedgehogs have fifteen stiff spines to every square centimetre of their body.

16

The Romans divided the day into sixteen equal parts, each of ninety minutes.

Hernando Cortes introduced horses – eleven stallions and five mares – into Mexico in the sixteenth century. They bred in large numbers and were soon dispersed northwards into America, where they were eventually acquired by Indians through capture or trading.

There are sixteen lakes in the Lake District of north-west England within a radius of 30 miles (48 km). Windermere, the largest and most famous, is over 10 miles (16 km) long.

The population density of West Germany (640 people to 1 sq mile; 2·59 sq km) is sixteen times higher than that of East Germany.

A Macedonian phalanx was a line of battle in which a body of troops, sixteen rows deep, were drawn in close array, with over-lapping shields.

Every day an average of sixteen people are killed on Britain's roads.

Broadway, the best known thoroughfare in New York, is also the longest at 16 miles (25·7 km).

Switzerland is sixteen times the size of its neighbour Luxembourg.

A sixteenth of a note is better known as a semiquaver.

On 21 June the longest day of the year, both London and Paris enjoy sixteen hours of daylight.

17

An American cicada, a shrill-chirping insect, spends seventeen years underground before emerging as an adult.

A snail travels at 4 m (13 ft) an hour. In other words it would take seventeen days for it to cover a mile (1·6 km).

At its narrowest point, Dover to Cap Gris Nez, the English Channel is only 17 miles (27 km) wide.

The highest rating on the Beaufort scale is 17 – the assessment for winds of 126–136 mph (202–218 kph).

In the UK convicted persons under the age of seventeen are tried by juvenile courts.

The Book of Genesis informs us that the Flood began on the seventeenth day of the second month, that after 150 days the waters had abated, and that on the seventeenth day of the seventh month the Ark of Noah came to rest on Mount Ararat.

Seventeen fully grown trees are required to provide just 1 tonne of paper for disposable bags.

Placed end to end, the roads of France would encircle the world seventeen times.

There are seventeen sapphires adding their own particular brilliance to St Edward's Crown, which the Queen wore at her Coronation in 1953. They are complemented by 2,783 diamonds, eleven emeralds and five rubies!

Queen Elizabeth II is Head of State of seventeen countries, including the world's second largest – Canada.

18

In the UK an eighteen-year-old person can vote in local and general elections, can marry without the consent of parents, can make a will, and can sue or be sued.

In 1829 George Shillibeer introduced London's first omnibus, with seating for eighteen passengers.

A horse has eighteen pairs of ribs; a human being has twelve.

In 1858 the Virgin Mary was said to have appeared eighteen times within a fortnight before the illiterate fourteen-year-old Bernadette Soubirous at the grotto of Massabielle in Lourdes, south-west France. It has since become a place of mass pilgrimage, and many miracle cures have been claimed.

2 November 1982 marked the start of Channel 4 – the first new British television service for eighteen years.

Used mainly for wedding rings, 18-carat gold is 75 per cent pure gold and 25 per cent copper.

Lester Piggott was only eighteen when he rode his first Derby winner, Never Say Die, in 1954.

Dogs common in one country can be extremely rare in another. For example, there are only eighteen English foxhounds in the entire USA.

Enrico Caruso (1873–1921), the eighteenth child in a poor Neapolitan family of twenty, was the first to survive infancy. He became the greatest and most famous tenor the world has ever known.

A clarinet, known for its full, sweet and mellow tone, consists basically of a wooden tube pierced by eighteen holes, half of which are closed by the fingers and the other nine by keys. Its range is similar to that of a violin.

19

There are over 19,000 churches in the UK.

Delusions, hallucinations and hearing the voice of God are among the nineteen recognized symptoms of schizophrenia.

New York can fairly claim to be the most cosmopolitan city in the world. In 1970, almost 19% of its 18 million inhabitants had been born abroad.

Eye test charts use nineteen letters arranged in seven groups of capital letters of different sizes.

In 1970 the American dare-devil motor-cyclist Evel Knievel established a world record by clearing nineteen cars – a distance of 39 m (43 yd) – at the Ontario Motor Speedway, California, before a crowd of 70,000.

It took only nineteen months to erect the 381 m (1,250 ft) Empire State Building in New York, which was officially opened on 1 March 1931.

The Earth is moving on its path around the sun at about 19 miles (30 km) per second. Feeling dizzy?

The 1964 Tokyo Olympic flame was ignited by nineteen-year-old Yoshinori Sakai who was born in Hiroshima just an hour before the atomic bomb exploded in 1945.

In 1497 277 men embarked in five ships on Ferdinand Magellan's historic expedition around the world. In 1499 just nineteen men returned in the *Vittoria*, sadly without their leader.

The first woman to swim the English Channel was the nineteen-year-old American Gertrude Ederle on 6 August 1926. She crossed from Cap Gris-Nez to Dover in fourteen hours, thirty-nine minutes, and it soon became apparent that her hearing had been permanently impaired.

A two-and-a-half-year-old child should have acquired all its twenty milk teeth.

20

A French culinary treat is a fish stew called bouillabaisse, which originated in Marseilles, a Mediterranean seaport. It contains no less than twenty kinds of fish and is very spicy.

The human skeleton represents 20 per cent – one-fifth – of our body weight.

The speed limit on roads in the UK was only 20 mph (32 kph) until 1930.

Only 300 years ago there were twenty times as many trees in the UK as there are today.

The American author Washington Irving (1783–1859) is best remembered as the creator of that delightful character Rip Van Winkle, who slept for two decades.

Anne Boleyn was given £20 on 19 May 1536, the day of her execution, to distribute to the imported French swordsman and his assistants as payment for their gruesome task!

Paris is a very compact city bounded by a ring road – the *Périphérique* – and is divided into twenty arrondissements or districts which spiral out from the centre.

A two-and-a-half-year-old child should have acquired all its twenty milk teeth.

The Eiffel Tower in Paris can sway as much as 20 cm (8 in) in a strong wind.

The world's largest variety of fruit, the double coconut, indigenous to the Seychelles in the Indian Ocean, weighs about 20 kg (44 lb). It takes ten years to ripen.

21

Onion, garlic, clove, paprika, cinnamon, chili, ginger and poppy seed are just some of the twenty-one spices which might be present in a good curry.

The lighthouse at the Lizard, Cornwall, has a beam visible for 21 miles (33·8 km). It gives a white flash every three seconds, and has saved countless ships from being wrecked on the rugged rocks nearby.

It takes twenty-one days from the start of incubation for a chick to hatch.

Popular legend has it that the gunfighter and outlaw Bill the Kid (William H. Bonney) (1859–81) murdered twenty-one men, one for each of his years, but there is no proof of this. He shot two deputies in escaping from Lincoln County jail and was hunted down and finally killed by a former friend, sheriff Pat Garrett.

Buck-toothed Goofy – one of Walt Disney's best-loved cartoon characters – made his screen debut in *Mickey's Revue* (1932) and endured for twenty-one years.

The value of a golden guinea was fixed at twenty-one shillings in 1717.

Roman Catholics over twenty-one are obliged to refrain from eating meat on all Fridays in Lent.

In 1960 National Service conscription for men in the UK finally ended after a period of twenty-one years.

When London's Big Ben was monitored for accuracy some years ago, it was found to have been wrong on only twenty-one occasions over a period of 288 days. Even then the error was never more than a second!

Coral reefs only develop in areas where the sea's temperature never falls below 21°C (70°F). The three principal kinds are atolls, fringing reefs and barrier reefs. The Great Barrier Reef off north-east Australia is rapidly being eaten away by a genus of starfish called the Crown of Thorns.

22

A milk bottle is likely to be re-used some twenty-two times.

Twenty-two per cent of human bone is water.

Only twenty-two players competed in the first ever Men's Singles Championship at Wimbledon in 1877.

The Queen is colonel-in-chief (or captain-general) of twenty-two British regiments.

At the command of William I, twenty-two Saxon villages in what is now the county of Hampshire were razed by the Normans to make an enlarged royal hunting ground. Tree-planting began in 1079, and the area was called the New Forest.

For Frenchmen the highlight of the sporting season is the Tour de France cycling race. The riders cover a distance of about 2,485 miles (4,000 km) divided into twenty-two daily laps, the winner of each being entitled to wear the famous yellow jersey.

The British prime minister heads a cabinet of twenty-two senior ministers.

If exposed to a temperature of −30°C (−22°F) in a 22 mph (35 kph) wind, inactive human flesh would freeze in just one minute.

Twenty-two million people inhabit the islands of the Pacific.

The popular Spanish golfer Severiano Ballesteros was only twenty-two when he won the 1979 British Open – the youngest champion this century.

23

Of the thirty-nine men who have been US presidents, twenty-three have been lawyers.

There are twenty-three courts at the Old Bailey, more formally known as the Central Criminal Court, London; No 1 has been the scene of many celebrated cases.

The British government is spending £23 million a year on constructing deep shelters from which to govern in case of a nuclear attack.

The twenty-third modern Olympiad took place at Los Angeles, California, in July/August 1984, when the USA played host to 140 of the member nations of the Olympic movement.

On average a murder is committed every twenty-three minutes in the USA.

Landseer's four bronze lions were added to the pedestal of Nelson's Column in 1867, some twenty-three years after its original unveiling in London's Trafalgar Square.

During 1984 an estimated 23 million babies were born in India.

On their return from the moon in July 1969, the crew of *Apollo 11* found themselves in great demand. Messrs Armstrong, Aldrin and Collins addressed Congress, received Medals of Freedom, paraded through US cities and toured no less than twenty-three countries.

The most familiar and most beautiful of the 150 psalms of the Old Testament is surely the 23rd, which begins: 'The Lord is my shepherd . . .'

The magnificent East window of England's largest Gothic cathedral, York Minster, is 23·7 m (78 ft) high – the length of a tennis court! It is filled with 117 panels, each depicting a scene from the Bible, from Creation to Judgment.

24

In golf the handicap limit for men is twenty-four.

Blue Peter is the name of a hugely popular BBC television programme for children. It is also a blue flag with a white central square which is hoisted twenty-four hours before a ship leaves harbour.

Prince Charles is the twenty-fourth Duke of Cornwall. He succeeded to the title on 6 February 1952, when he was three!

The eggs of the common housefly hatch within twenty-four hours, but only if the temperature is 24°C (75°F) or above.

There are never at any one time more than twenty-four Knights of the Garter. This is one of the greatest honours the British monarch can bestow on her subjects.

Ephemera are insects such as the mayfly who have a life-span of only twenty-four hours or less.

The *Odyssey* is an epic poem in twenty-four books, usually attributed to the blind Greek poet Homer (ninth century BC). It tells the story of the homecoming after ten years of wandering of Odysseus (known also as Ulysses), King of Ithaca.

Twenty-four sheets of paper make a quire.

The cables used in the Golden Gate Bridge, San Francisco, weigh 24,384 tonne (24,000 ton).

Seven equilateral triangles, all with the same measurements, can be placed together to make twenty-four different shapes.

25

Under British law there are twenty-five close relations that a man or woman is forbidden to marry.

London has twenty-five pearly royal families, each belonging to a different district. They do charity work and are seen at Easter parades in full regalia.

There are 25 miles (40 km) of carpets on the *QE 2*.

First planned in the 1930s, the M25, London's 121 mile (195 km) orbital road skirting the busy city and suburbs, is due for completion in 1986.

In 1977 London Transport had twenty-five of its normally red Routemaster buses repainted silver to honour the Queen's Silver Jubilee.

A length in swimming measures 25 m (82 ft).

Study a page of stamps or a Georgian window. You will see that twenty-five is the smallest number of squares which can be completely surrounded by an even smaller number of squares (twenty-four).

A temperature of 25°C (77°F) is the highest ever recorded in the Falkland Islands.

On 15 December 1783, the Frenchman Jean-François Pilatre de Rozier became the first man to make an ascent in a hot air balloon. It reached an anchored height of 25·6 m (84 ft).

Lake Rotoroa on the North Island of New Zealand plunges to a depth of 25·6 m (84 ft) and was probably created by a huge volcanic explosion. Geysers of boiling mud and tall columns of hot water and steam have made it a major tourist attraction.

26

The golden hamster can breed after only twenty-six days, a record among vertebrates.

The average year of the Gregorian calendar, even with leap years, is about twenty-six seconds longer than it takes the Earth to complete its orbit round the Sun. However, it would take 3,323 years for this slight discrepancy to amount to a whole day.

A peanut is 26 per cent protein, and contains eleven of the thirteen minerals essential to human growth.

Twenty-six popes have had the misfortune to be assassinated.

George III was very proud of his collection of twenty-six copies of the ninety-six books printed by William Caxton.

The University Boat Race of 1860 was the slowest ever, with Cambridge winning in twenty-six minutes, that is nine more than Oxford needed for the fastest ever win in 1976.

After 1931, when he was sixty-six, the great Finnish composer Jean Sibelius never published another note of music in the remaining twenty-six years of his life. All inspiration had been drained.

Zoo-kept royal pythons, found in Ghana, can exist for twenty-six days without food.

In 490 BC the Greeks defeated the Persians at the Battle of Marathon, fought on a plain about 26 miles (41·8 km) from Athens. Over 6,000 Persians were killed for the loss of only 200 Greeks. The victorious news was brought to Athens by a runner called Pheidippides, who dropped dead with exhaustion after delivering his message. In 1908 the Olympic marathon distance was standardized at 26 miles 385 yd (42·1 km).

The Great Pyramid of Cheops in Egypt is at 137 m (450 ft) 26 m (85 ft) higher than St Paul's Cathedral, London.

27

For comfort the back seats of cars should be inclined at an angle of 27° from the upright.

Brigham Young (1801–77), who succeeded the sect's founder, Joseph Smith, as president of the Mormon Church, practised polygamy and took twenty-seven wives.

In 1985 only twenty-seven of Britain's 10,800 bank managers were women.

When only twenty-seven years old, J. M. W. Turner, the great British artist, was made a full Royal Academician (RA) – one of the youngest ever and half John Constable's age at his election.

Anne Hathaway was twenty-seven when she married the nineteen-year-old William Shakespeare in 1583. Her cottage can still be visited in the village of Shottery, just outside Stratford-upon-Avon.

Twenty-seven cities in the USA have a population in excess of a million.

In 1948 Oslo, Norway's modest capital, suddenly grew twenty-seven times bigger in size, when large areas of surrounding countryside were brought within the city's boundaries.

Citizens' Band is a short-wave radio service, popular with drivers of vehicles as a two-way method of communication. The radio frequency used is 27 megahertz, and it has a range of 5–15 miles (8–24 km).

The craze of 1978 was a cube invented by the Hungarian architect Erno Rubik to help teach three-dimensional design. The wooden or plastic hexahedron consists of twenty-seven small cubes fastened together. The object of the game is to see how quickly the player can get the nine small faces on each of the six sides all of the same colour.

The Roman army consisted of twenty-seven legions. Each legion had a force of about 6,000 men, including 120 cavalry, and an eagle as a standard.

28

Out of every twenty-eight British engineers only one is a woman.

A set of dominoes consists of twenty-eight pieces.

Gaunt-faced English actor Boris Karloff (1887–1969) went to Hollywood and achieved world fame as the monster in *Frankenstein* in 1931. He starred in twenty-eight 'monster' films in all, including *The Mummy*, *The Mask of Fu Manchu*, *House of Frankenstein* and *The Body Snatchers*.

In 1981 Easter Sunday and the Jewish Feast of the Passover coincided. This happens every twenty-eight years – the next occasion will be in 2009.

Many animals feed on grass which contains twenty-eight times more of each vitamin (with the exception of vitamin D) than all known vegetables.

The USA is over twenty-eight times the size of its recent adversary, Vietnam.

On average twenty-eight children worldwide die from malnutrition every minute.

There were twenty-eight beads on a Roman abacus, which was used for counting.

Tin Pan Alley is the popular name for 28th Street in New York City where earlier this century most of the commercial songs were published.

To make cheese the milk of cows, goats or sheep must be heated to 28°C (83°F).

29

For twenty-nine years, from 1934 until 1963, Alcatraz on Pelican Island in San Francisco Bay was one of America's grimmest high-security prisons. Nobody ever escaped alive.

Britain produces 29 million tonne (28.6 million ton) of rubbish every year – enough to fill Wembley Stadium ten times!

A baby is born with twenty-nine small bones in its skull. Eight of them slowly fuse together to form the cranium which protects the brain.

During World War II 29,890 people lost their lives through enemy action in London.

Each parliamentary session at Westminster twenty-nine days are set apart on which the topic for debate is chosen by the official Opposition.

West Berlin is bigger than East Berlin by 29 sq miles (75 sq km).

It takes Saturn 29½ Earth years to orbit the sun.

It is the ambition of all British scientists to be admitted to the Royal Society, which has flourished for over 300 years. Each year only twenty-nine newcomers are accepted as members.

The oldest lion in captivity was Nero, who was twenty-nine when he died in Cologne City Zoo in 1908.

The lowest elevation in the whole of Europe and Asia is the Caspian Sea, which except for its southern shore lies within the Soviet Union. It is an incredible 29 m (96 ft) below sea level.

The stratosphere, where the temperature is freezing point (0°C; 32°F), is approximately 30 miles (50 km) above the Earth's surface.

30

The hour hand of a clock face turns through an angle of 30° every hour.

During World War II British and Commonwealth air crews earned a temporary rest after completing a 'tour' of thirty missions against the enemy.

Thirty muscles control the fingers of each hand.

A modern construction firm – Wimpey's – believe that they could build a replica Stonehenge (now 4,000 years old) at a cost of £332,640. Instead of the original 1,000 labourers, they estimate that a workforce of thirty could do the job!

There are thirty meteor craters located on Earth. The largest astrobleme 8½ miles (13·7 km) wide near Deep Bay, Saskatchewan, in Canada, was discovered in 1956–57.

Couples celebrating a pearl wedding anniversary will have been married for thirty years.

The stratosphere, where the temperature is freezing point (0°C; 32°F), is approximately 30 miles (50 km) above the Earth's surface.

Harrow, one of the top British public schools, whose past pupils included Byron, Sheridan, Peel, Palmerston and Churchill, was founded in 1571 by a local yeoman called John Lyons for 'thirty poor children of the parish of Harrow'.

The common housefly can transmit around thirty diseases.

The giant bamboo, native to Asia, can grow 30 m (98 ft) in a single year – the equivalent height of seventeen men.

31

Howard Lee Hale of Virginia, USA, died on 10 May 1976, after having spent thirty-one years, nine months in an iron lung.

There are 31,536,000 seconds in 365 days.

Biffo the Bear was featured weekly in the *Beano* comic for thirty-one years between 24 January 1948 and 14 November 1979.

The ever expanding chain of McDonald's restaurants – 8,000 in thirty-one countries by 1984 – claims to sell 140 hamburgers a second!

Some noble lines stretch back into obscurity. The present Countess of Mar, the thirty-first in succession, can trace her ancestors back to 1115.

Twice a year in Britain and most other European countries the clocks are moved forward or backward an hour in order to ensure the maximum amount of daylight. Since 1964 British Summer Time (BST) has lasted thirty-one weeks, beginning in March and ending in October.

A well-known prophecy is that a rainy St Swithin's day (15 July) will begin a wet spell lasting forty days. In 1848 it remained dry on the day in question, but rained heavily on thirty-one of the following forty days!

When Charles II reclaimed his throne in 1660, he found that the set of regalia had been melted down on Oliver Cromwell's orders. The cost of a new crown, orb, sword and sceptre was £31,978 9s 11d.

A distance of only 31 miles (50 km) separates the two Lancashire industrial cities of Liverpool and Manchester.

The midday temperature at Lugh Gunane in Somalia, East Africa, has never been known to fall below 31°C (88°F).

32

The brilliant scientist and mathematician Sir Isaac Newton (1642–1727) once made a fortune of £32,000 speculating on the Stock Exchange.

Pius IX (born 1792), who was pope for a record thirty-two years (1846–78), was one of the most influential. It was he who proclaimed the dogma of the Immaculate Conception in 1854 and that of Papal Infallibility in 1870.

What is a book? By government definition a book consists of at least thirty-two pages of printed words, twenty-four in the case of poetry.

'Boxing the compass' is a term used to describe naming the thirty-two points or directions marked on a ship's compass.

Dr Theodor Morell, Hitler's personal physician from 1936 to 1945, treated him with thirty-two different drugs for a wide range of ailments.

The property department at Covent Garden Opera House, London, has at its disposal 32,000 wigs for opera and ballet.

About 3 million Parisians are crowded into an area of only 32 sq miles (82·8 sq km), making the French capital the most densely populated city in Europe.

Just imagine a bicycle 18 m (59 ft) long. Such a machine, capable of being ridden by thirty-two people simultaneously, was constructed in England in 1974.

When a young man, the famous lexicographer Samuel Johnson frequently walked the muddy road from his birthplace, Lichfield, to Birmingham and back in a day – a distance of 32 miles (51·5 km).

The world's first crossword puzzle was published in the *New York World* on 21 December 1913. It was compiled by Arthur Wyane from Liverpool, who provided thirty-two clues.

33

The most famous of English flat races, the Epsom Derby, is run over a course of 1½ miles (2·4 km) and is limited to thirty-three three-year-old colts.

Yorkshire have been English County Cricket Champions outright on thirty-one occasions, and joint winners in 1869 and 1949.

The person who starred in the most musical films – a record total of thirty-three – was Elvis Presley (1935–77).

The definition of a film short is one less than 914 m (3,000 ft), which would take about thirty-three minutes to show.

Trigger, the horse used by cowboy star Roy Rogers in a string of eighty-seven films between 1938 and 1953, died in 1965 at the age of thirty-three.

The Olympic torch finally arrived in Los Angeles on 21 July 1984, after a seventy-five day journey of 8,700 miles (14,000 km) through thirty-three US states.

Centre Point, the tall building overlooking the junction of New Oxford Street and Charing Cross Road in London, has thirty-three storeys, mostly still unoccupied.

Thirty-three countries made contributions towards the fine interior of the International Peace Palace in the Hague, Holland, where the famous Court of Justice meets.

Chicago can fairly claim to be the rail centre of the world with terminals for thirty-three trunk lines!

In 1946 the temperature reached 33°C (90°F) or more on 333 consecutive days at Wyndham, Western Australia – just about eleven months of glorious sunshine!

34

William Booth (1829–1912) was General of the Salvation Army, which he founded, from 1878 until his death thirty-four years later.

Prince Albert (later George VI, father of the present Queen) was born on 14 December 1895, the thirty-fourth anniversary of the Prince Consort's death in 1861, and was, therefore, given his name. Incidentally, Queen Victoria's second daughter, Princess Alice, died on the same fateful date in 1878.

The average journey on British Rail in 1983 was 34 miles (55 km).

Greater London measures 34 miles (55 km) across at its widest point.

Thirty-four per cent of British parents allow their children to have a television set in their own rooms.

Mormons, a religious sect of 5 million people, believe that Jesus Christ landed in America in AD 34 and preached a second ministry.

The first ever lighter-than-air transatlantic flight was made by the British dirigible R34 in 1919. The airship completed the crossing from the Firth of Forth, Scotland, to Long Island, USA, in 108 hours.

Queen Elizabeth I's fleet of thirty-four vessels successfully defeated King Philip II's Spanish Armada of 130 ships and twenty caravels in 1588.

Epping to West Ruislip on the Central line, a distance of 34·1 miles (55 km), is the longest journey possible without the need to change trains on the London underground system.

Cecil William Mercer, better known as Dornford Yates, (1885–1960) wrote thirty-four thrilling adventure books, mostly involving the Secret Service.

35

There are 35,000 licensed taxis and twice that number of drivers in Britain. London's share is 12,500 cabs and 17,000 drivers.

Gallup polls, founded in 1935, are widely used in thirty-five countries throughout the world to test public opinion. British outlets are the *Daily Telegraph* and *Sunday Telegraph*.

The maximum speed limit on the Channel Island of Guernsey is 35 mph (56 kph).

As much as 35 per cent of heat can escape through the walls of an uninsulated house.

Between 1980, when he made his professional debut, and 1984, the three times world snooker champion Steve Davis won an incredible thirty-five titles, and in the process became the sport's first millionaire.

Napoleon's troops occupied Moscow for only thirty-five days in August/September 1812 before beginning an ignominious retreat. The fleeing Russians had set fire to the city, and there was meagre food, not much shelter and appalling weather conditions to contend with.

Sir Richard Burton (1821–90) was a remarkable Victorian explorer, travel writer and translator. He spoke thirty-five languages, including Hindustani, Persian, Portuguese and Arabic, and when he was only fourteen he became the first known white man to enter the holy city of Mecca, which is forbidden to non-Moslems.

Nobody under 35 years of age can become President of the USA.

St Peter's Basilica in Rome, the world's largest church, is as high as a thirty-five storey building.

The mean temperature of the sun is 35 million°C (63 million°F).

36

The Gospels of Matthew, Mark, Luke and John recount thirty-six miracles performed by Jesus, none, incidentally, for his own benefit.

The last trams to be seen in London ran on the No 36 route along the Thames Embankment until 5 July 1952.

On 5 September 1885, Arbroath beat the visiting team of Bon Accord (who played in studless boots on a muddy pitch) 36–0 in the Scottish Cup. This remains today the record score in a first-class British soccer match.

The great Australian swimmer Dawn Fraser broke thirty-six world records. Her string of victories in the Women's 100-m freestyle in the 1956, 1960 and 1964 Olympic Games is still unequalled.

A pair of rabbits could in thirty-six months produce 13,718,000 descendants!

The thirty-six remaining inhabitants of lonely St Kilda in the Outer Hebrides, Scotland, were evacuated in 1930 at their own request, leaving the island as a paradise for birds.

Matthew Webb's achievement of swimming the English Channel in 1875 was not repeated until thirty-six years later when, in 1911, the Yorkshireman Thomas Burgess made the crossing. It took the French aviator Louis Blériot thirty-six minutes, thirty seconds to fly from Calais to Dover on 25 July 1909, to become the first pilot to cross the Channel.

Ships of all nations use the International Code of Flag Signals. There are thirty-six flags in all, one for each of the twenty-six letters of the English alphabet, and a further ten to embrace the numbers 0 to 9. They are raised in hoists of up to five flags to spell words or code signals.

Thirty-six is the only number between 0 and 100 which is a square (6×6), a rectangle (3×12) and triangle $(1+2+3+4+5+6+7+8)$ number.

The normal temperature of a human body is 36·9°C (98·4°F).

37

Thirty-seven per cent of British men play some kind of sport.

In the list of Mozart symphonies (1 to 41) there is no Symphony No 37.

A roulette table carries a revolving wheel divided into thirty-seven compartments numbered 0 to 36. The numbers do not follow any particular order, but eighteen are black, another eighteen are red, and O is green. Only hymns numbered from thirty-seven upward are sung these days at the English church in Monte Carlo following the discovery that worshippers were inclined to place their bets at the casino on the numbers chosen by the priest, no doubt hoping for divine inspiration.

There are thirty-seven motorways in the UK, though some of them are still unfinished.

There are thirty-seven marquesses, British nobles next in rank to dukes.

World War I broke out on 4 August 1914, just thirty-seven days after the assassination in Sarajevo of the Archduke Franz Ferdinand, heir to the throne of Austria, by a Bosnian fanatic.

Exhausted by work, the brilliant Renaissance artist Raphael – noted for his Madonna and Child compositions and frescoes – died in 1520 on his thirty-seventh birthday.

There are thirty-seven members of the dog family.

Mount Everest 8,848 m (29,028 ft) is the highest of the thirty-seven peaks in Asia over 7,468 m (24,500 ft).

At her death in 1901 Queen Victoria already had thirty-seven surviving great-grandchildren.

38

During the six years from 1948 to 1954 the 'Czech flyer', Emil Zatopek, was never beaten in thirty-eight consecutive 10,000-m races – a phenomenal achievement. He won four Olympic Gold medals and set eighteen new world record times.

By law British state schools must open for a minimum of 380 half days – in other words, for thirty-eight weeks.

The shortest war in which Britain has ever been involved was a thirty-eight minute trial of strength against Zanzibar, East Africa, in 1896.

A Bible printed in Braille requires thirty-eight volumes and weighs 60 kg (132 lb).

The biggest jail break in British history occurred as recently as 25 September 1983, when thirty-eight IRA terrorist prisoners escaped from the Maze high-security prison in Belfast.

Near the town of Jackson, Mississippi, USA is the famous Petrified Forest, consisting of giant fossilized trees dating back 38 million years!

The first rules for bare knuckle fighting were drawn up by the English champion Jack Broughton (1705–89). A round ended when one of the fighters was knocked down. If he failed to regain his feet within thirty-eight seconds, his opponent would be declared the winner.

Heathrow, London's major airport, can handle 38 million passengers a year.

There are 38,000 kinds of mushrooms and toadstools.

The first commercial telegraph line linked the US cities of Washington and Baltimore, a distance of 38 miles (61 km). The historic opening message relayed on 24 May 1844 was simply: 'What hath God wrought'.

39

There were thirty-nine episodes of the highly successful and oft repeated BBC television series *Steptoe and Son* (1964–74). Wilfred Brambell and Harry H. Corbett starred as the widowed rag-and-bone dealer and his bachelor son.

The sport of speedway was introduced into England from Australia at High Beech, Loughton, Essex, in 1928. There are now thirty-nine league teams in Britain.

A Eurocheque card can be used in over 180,000 banks and 4·5 million shops, hotels, restaurants and petrol stations in thirty-nine countries.

The United Nations Secretariat Building in New York City is made of steel and is thirty-nine storeys high. Its 5,400 blue-green windows are kept clean by a permanent staff of nine.

Mercury, a liquid metal, will solidify at a temperature of −39°C (−38°F).

In 1921, when he was only thirty-nine, Franklin Delano Roosevelt (1882–1945) was crippled with polio and never walked unaided again. However, so strong was his resolve that he became the thirty-second and longest serving US president, holding office from 1931 until 1945.

The population of the world should double within thirty-nine years, from 4·8 billion people to 9·6 billion!

For thirty-nine most industrious and productive years the Austrian composer Joseph Haydn (1732–1809) was musical director at the court of Prince Nicholas Esterhazy. However, despite his eminence, he was treated like a servant.

Greyhounds can reach a speed of 39 mph (63 kph).

Florence Nightingale headed a party of thirty-nine nurses who went to Scutari, Turkey, at the outbreak of the Crimean War in 1854 to aid the sick and wounded. Within six months better hygiene and the use of antiseptics had reduced the death toll in the hospital from 42 per cent to just 2 per cent. A remarkable achievement.

The North African Ostrich lays eggs about 17·8 cm (7 in) long. It takes forty minutes to boil one!

40

Forty per cent of British people still believe that religion is an essential part of life.

Forty members is the minimum number required to form a quorum for debate in the House of Commons.

Ascension Day – Holy Thursday – is the fortieth day after Easter Sunday. It commemorates the ascent of Jesus into Heaven.

The fortieth Archbishop of Canterbury was Saint Thomas Becket (1118–70), whose quarrels with the king led to four knights taking it upon themselves to slay him in his cathedral.

It takes 40,000 years for a substance to completely lose its radioactivity.

The North African ostrich lays eggs about 17·8 cm (7 in) long. It takes forty minutes to boil one!

There are forty kinds of ladybird in Britain. They range from the familiar 2 and 7 spotted varieties to those with 9, 11, 22 and even 24 spots.

To construct just one mile (1·6 km) of motorway eats up 40 acres (16·2 hectares) of land.

During World War II (1939–45) German armies twice came within 40 miles (64 km) of the Russian capital, Moscow.

For forty years until his death, Lord Burghley (William Cecil, 1520–98) was Queen Elizabeth I's Secretary of State – 'the power behind the throne'.

41

Forty-one per cent of British savings are now invested in banks.

The remarkable surrealist paintings of the eccentric Spanish artist Salvador Dali hang in forty-one of the world's principal art galleries.

Forty-one per cent of the UK's population of 55·5 million are adults – that is, eighteen or over.

In September, 1939, the upper age limit for conscription of men into the Armed Forces was forty-one, and it remained so for the duration of World War II.

When he was forty-one the German-born composer George Friderick Handel (1685–1759) became a British subject.

Saint Augustine was the leader of a party of forty-one monks who landed at Ebbsfleet, Kent, in AD 597 with the aim of converting the Anglo-Saxons to Christianity.

Battling Nelson floored his opponent Christy Williams a record forty-one times before winning in the seventeenth round of a fight at Hot Springs, Arkansas, USA, on Boxing Day, 1902.

Forty-one gun salutes are reserved for the birth of royal children, and for when the Queen in person opens, prorogues or dissolves Parliament, or passes through London in procession.

In the summer of 1979 a Majorcan farmer Tomeo Estranary had the good fortune to pick a 7·7 kg (17 lb) mushroom. When cooked, it made an excellent meal for forty-one neighbours and members of his family.

By 1943 better protection for convoys and more sophisticated radar enabled the Allies to destroy during March of that year forty-one U-boats – the worst loss of the entire war.

42

At forty-two, Theodore Roosevelt (1858–1919) became the youngest of all US presidents, when in 1901 he succeeded William McKinley who had been assassinated.

Carl Lewis, the black athlete who won four Gold medals at the 1984 Olympic Games in Los Angeles, is the subject of sports writer John Devany's book *Carl! The Story of an American Hero*, which went on sale in Chicago just forty-two hours after its completion.

Of the forty-two countries who joined the League of Nations at Geneva in 1919, thirteen had been neutral in World War I.

There are now forty-two oil-drilling rigs in the North Sea bringing liquid gold ashore for Britain.

All births in the UK must be notified to the local registrar within forty-two days.

The spy George Blake was given the longest prison sentence ever imposed under British law – forty-two years. He was 'sprung' from Wormwood Scrubs in October 1966, after serving only sixty-five months, and now lives in the Soviet Union.

There are 42 million blind people in the world.

With only a few rare exceptions, canines have forty-two teeth. Get your dog to stand still while you count!

Debenhams, a department store on London's Oxford Street, has welcome signs in forty-two languages.

The ancient Egyptians were convinced that forty-two demons were present at the last judgment of every human being. The number represented the districts of Egypt, so that at least one demon could claim an individual's soul from personal knowledge of his past life in his home district.

43

The uniquely gifted Greek soprano Maria Callas (1923–77) gave over 500 stage performances in forty-three operatic roles.

All vehicles over three years old have to be examined annually under Section 43 of the Road Traffic Act of 1972 – in other words, the MOT test!

Forty-three per cent of a human body is muscle.

Unless they are in intense pain, 43 per cent of British adults do not visit a dentist.

Over 43,000 people are at present confined in British prisons.

Forty-three per cent of the working population of the UK are employed in industry.

London's worst ever underground disaster occurred on 28 February 1975, when at 8.46 a.m. a Northern line train ploughed into the wall at the end of the tunnel at Moorgate, killing forty-three and injuring seventy-four.

The ideal temperature for a hot bath is 43°C (110°F).

My Word, the popular radio game begun in 1956 by the comedy team of Frank Muir and Dennis Norden, is heard in forty-three countries.

Maria Peron was 43 in 1974 when she became the world's first female president – of Argentina. John F. Kennedy was the same age when he became the first Catholic president of the USA in 1960.

44

About 44 per cent of white people have blood group O.

Coventry City used a total of forty-four players during the 1919–20 soccer season, and this remains an England Football League record.

The front sprocket wheel of a bicycle has forty-four little teeth which engage the links of the chain. The back sprocket has only half as many, so therefore the wheels will turn twice for every revolution of the pedals. Clever!

The once very popular Initial Teaching Alphabet (ITA), introduced by Sir James Pitman in 1959 to assist early reading, has forty-four characters whose pronunciation never changes.

The 44 acres (17·7 hectares) of Kennington Oval, the home of Surrey county cricket club, is part of the Duchy of Cornwall, and thus one of the many properties belonging to the Prince of Wales.

When the people of Gibraltar were given the choice in 1967 of remaining linked to Britain or changing to Spanish rule, only forty-four out of the 12,000 who voted were in favour of the latter.

Forty-four thousand florists in 130 countries have connections with Interflora, which specializes in the speedy delivery of flowers for all occasions.

Aristophanes (*c* 445–385 BC), the greatest of Greek comedy writers, produced forty-four plays. The eleven to survive include *Wasps*, *Lysistrata* and *Clouds*, which are still performed today.

The US space shuttles have forty-four reaction control engines. These thrusters can be fired singly or in pairs, and make possible maximum control over direction and altitude, besides coping with changes of pitch, yaw or roll in space.

It was not until forty-four years after the tragic death in 1912 of Captain Scott and his companions that humans next arrived at the South Pole, since when it has become a base for American meteorological research.

45

Some street names are very popular, and in London ninety-seven of them are used at least twelve times, and there are no fewer than forty-five High Streets and forty-five Park Roads.

There were forty-five vineyards in fourteen of England's southern counties, according to the Domesday survey of 1086. By 1967 the number had increased to 105, and some English table wines are now highly regarded by the experts.

A recent piece of research (the Cockcroft Report) indicates that forty-five per cent of British adults are baffled by the 24 hour-clock timetable.

Scotland has forty-five malt whisky distilleries.

John Wilkes (1727–97) published a violent attack on George III's speech to parliament in 1763. It was printed in the notorious issue No 45 of the magazine *The North Briton*, and resulted in Wilkes and others being arrested for libel.

Jackie Milburn had the ball in the net a record forty-five seconds after the kick-off in Newcastle's 3–1 win over Manchester City in the 1955 FA Cup Final at Wembley!

Every year 45 tonne (44·3 ton) of paint are lavished on the skeletal frame of the Eiffel Tower in Paris.

King Louis XIV of France (1638–1715) was forty-five when he took as his second wife Madame de Maintenon, who had been governess to his children by Queen Marie-Thérèse.

A cubit was an ancient measure 45·7 cm (18 in) long, based on the length of the forearm of an adult male.

A 45 kg (100 lb) capybara can be reduced to a skeleton in less than a minute by a shoal of piranha.

46

A tablespoon of sugar contains 46 calories of energy.

The minimum weight for medium-size eggs is 46 g (1⅝ oz).

George Friderick Handel (1685–1759), in addition to his many oratorios, composed forty-six operas, the first being *Almira* in 1705, and the last *Deidamia* in 1741.

A standard milk churn will hold 46 litres (10 gal).

Leslie Charteris wrote forty-six immensely popular thrillers featuring Simon Templar, the Saint, a kind of gentleman Robin Hood acting outside the law. Louis Hayward, George Sanders and Roger Moore have all played the part in films or television.

Oscar Hammerstein (1895–1960) wrote the words and many memorable lyrics for forty-six musical shows. Among his collaborators were Romberg, Gershwin, Youmans, Friml and Rodgers.

William, the lovable eleven-year-old rascal of the Just William books, was created by Richmal Crompton, who died in 1969. He appeared in over thirty-six books over a span of forty-six years, beginning with the publication of *The Outlaw* in 1922.

The forty-six original Knights of the Bath were created at the coronation of Henry IV, who reigned from 1399 until 1413.

San Francisco claims to have forty-six parks.

London's oldest inn 'The Hoop and Grapes' in Aldgate was within 46 m (50 yd) of being consumed in the Great Fire of 1666.

47

The Soviet Union is allowed to have forty-seven diplomats in the UK.

Famous for its carillon of forty-seven bells, the Westerkirk in Amsterdam is immensely popular with tourists as the final resting place of Holland's greatest painter, Rembrandt (1600–69), though nobody can identify the exact spot!

Only 7,500 people actually live in the City of London, but over 352,000 – forty-seven times that number – work there.

Sadly there are only forty-seven complete piers left in Britain, compared with eighty-five in 1900.

Forty-seven per cent of British women wear size 16 clothes or over.

It took forty-seven years for the Académie Française to publish in 1982 just the initial volume of its new edition of the French dictionary!

At the behest of James I, forty-seven scholars and divines worked in six groups between 1604 and 1611 on the Authorized Version of the Bible.

The Duke of Edinburgh was awarded the Order of Merit – a gift of the sovereign – on 10 June 1968, his forty-seventh birthday.

For forty-seven years (1867–1914) the ruler of Egypt was known as the khedive, a Turkish word meaning viceroy.

To Pythagoras, a Greek philosopher of the sixth century BC, is attributed the proof of the 47th Proposition of the First Book of Euclid – that in a right-angled triangle the square of the hypotenuse is equal to the sum of the squares of the other two sides e.g. $3^2+4^2=5^2$, and $6^2+8^2=10^2$.

48

Fruit farmers generally plant forty-eight apple trees to the acre (0·4 hectare).

Forty-eight per cent of Jews living in Israel were born there.

Five million people made use of Britain's forty-eight private railways during the summer of 1984.

A potato has forty-eight chromosomes – the cells which determine appearance – two more than humans!

There are 48,000 factories in Tokyo, Japan.

A fully loaded milk float carries forty-eight crates, with twenty bottles in each crate.

The cat food Whiskas, a product of Pedigree Petfoods, now has a 48 per cent share of the market, more than three times that of its nearest rival Kit-E-Kat.

The writing, posting and receiving of letters earn forty-eight mentions in the Bible.

In 1847 the small Welsh town of Llandovery had forty-eight public houses to serve a population of only 1,709.

Dougie and Debbie Schee of Delaware, Ohio, USA must be the most unusual twins on record. Amazingly they were born forty-eight days apart in 1955.

49

There are forty-nine Anglican and twenty-one Roman Catholic cathedrals in England and Wales.

Former World Heavyweight Boxing Champion Rocky Marciano (1923–69) was undefeated in forty-nine fights between 2 February 1947 and his retirement on 27 April 1956.

Since 1979 the tallest office block in the UK has been the forty-nine storey National Westminster Tower (183 m; 600 ft) in Old Broad Street, London EC2.

Forty-nine US servicemen were sentenced to death for desertion during World War II, but only one, Private Eddie Slovik, was actually shot.

In England and Scotland it is against the law to sell deep sea oysters between 15 June and 4 August – a period of seven weeks or forty-nine days.

Bobby Charlton (Manchester United) holds the soccer-scoring record for England with forty-nine goals in 106 games between 1958 and 1970.

Forty-nine universities or institutions in the UK, including the Open University, can now confer academic degrees.

Arthur Prime, who began a life sentence in February 1969, and who is now an inmate of Sudbury Jail, has so far acquired forty-nine GCE passes (thirty-seven at O level and twelve at A level).

During a recent survey of the 49 acre (19·8 hectare) garden at Buckingham Palace, the botanist David Bellamy found that of 265 kinds of wild flowers present, fifty of them grow nowhere else in London.

In 1981 the difference between the average pay for men and women in Britain was £49 a week.

In April 1983, to celebrate the fiftieth anniversary of the classic film *King Kong* a 25·6 m (84 ft) balloon in the shape of a gorilla was hoisted up to the mooring mast of the Empire State Building in New York, inflated and left in position for a week.

50

The Venetian adventurer Casanova (1725–98), famous for his very revealing *Memoirs*, was given to breakfasting on fifty oysters.

For whistling at Marie-Amélie, the last Queen of France, the unfortunate Marquis de Pelier spent fifty years in prison.

Four British monarchs – Henry III, Edward III, George III and Queen Victoria – lived to celebrate their Golden Jubilee.

The London Philharmonic Orchestra repeated the introductory programme used by its founder Sir Thomas Beecham when it celebrated its fiftieth anniversary on 8 October 1982, at the Royal Festival Hall.

AC is short for alternating current, a flow of electricity which surges back and forth fifty times every second.

Every day there are two high tides about twelve hours, thirty minutes apart. They occur roughly fifty minutes later than those of the previous day.

An average of fifty children a month are killed or badly injured in transport accidents in the UK.

In 1984 Welshman Roger Rees triumphed as the fiftieth actor to play the part of Hamlet at the Royal Shakespeare Theatre in Stratford-upon-Avon.

In 1969 the seven-sided cupro-nickel fifty pence coin replaced the ten shilling note. It was designed by Christopher Ironside and weighs 13·5 g ($\frac{3}{5}$ oz).

In April 1983, to celebrate the fiftieth anniversary of the classic film *King Kong* a 25·6 m (84 ft) balloon in the shape of a gorilla was hoisted up to the mooring mast of the Empire State Building in New York, inflated and left in position for a week.

51

Fifty-one per cent of the population of the UK are female.

A seventeen-day Grand Tour of Yugoslavia in 1953 – Coronation Year – could be arranged for just £51.

There are an estimated 51 million hens in the UK.

The only British boxer to win the World Heavyweight Championship (1897) – besides the Middle (1891) and Light-Heavyweight (1903) crowns – was the Cornishman Bob Fitzsimmons, who was fifty-one and quite unmarked after his last fight!

King Gillette, an American with ambitions to perform a great service to all mankind, had sold only fifty-one of his newly patented safety razors by the end of 1902, and bankruptcy stared him in the face (clean-shaven, of course!). However, immense success came the following year with the introduction of the slotted blue blade.

Only fifty-one of the 262 popes have not been Italian.

Sherlock Holmes and Sexton Blake had a priestly rival for popularity when in 1911 the first of fifty-one Father Brown detective stories by G. K. Chesterton (1874–1936) was published with much acclaim.

London lies on latitude 51° 30′ N and longitude 0° 5′ W (almost the Greenwich Meridian).

When Elizabeth II came to the throne in 1952, Britain had a Queen as reigning monarch for the first time for fifty-one years after four successive kings.

In 1958 Boris Pasternak was awarded the fifty-first Nobel Prize for Literature for *Dr Zhivago*, but the Russian-born Novelist surprised the world by declining it.

52

The Mayas of Guatemala had a calendar based on a fifty-two year cycle.

There are fifty-two islands around the coast of Ireland.

In Australasia can be found fifty-two species of kangaroos and wallabies.

The greatest of all Test wicket-takers, with 4,187 victims between 1898 and 1930, was the Yorkshireman Wilfred Rhodes. He was 165 days past his fifty-second birthday – the oldest ever England player – when he took the field against the West Indies in Jamaica in 1930.

Not until 1857, fifty-two years after the Battle of Trafalgar, did ordinary seamen in the Royal Navy acquire a regulation uniform.

Only 52 per cent of British diplomats working abroad can speak French fluently.

There have been fifty-two kings of France, the last being Louis Philippe (overthrown in 1848). Margrethe II, Queen since 1972, is the fifty-second ruler of Denmark.

There are fifty-two breeds of domesticated rabbits.

Joggers or sponsored walk enthusiasts might like to note that the perimeter of Birmingham, England's second largest city, is 52 miles (84 km).

The final charge at the Battle of Waterloo in 1815 was made by the 52nd Light Infantry, so it seems unlikely that the Duke of Wellington actually spoke the words of incitement often ascribed to him, 'Up Guards and at 'em.'

53

There are fifty-three peaks over 4,267 m (14,000 ft) high and a further 831 between 3,353 m (11,000 ft) and 4,267 m (14,000 ft) in Colorado, USA. They form part of the Rocky Mountains.

Though church-going has declined, a surprising 53 per cent of Britain's population have been baptized.

The three great English industrial cities of Leeds, Manchester and Liverpool all lie on latitude 53°N.

White bread is 53 per cent carbohydrate in content.

It took fifty-three minutes for Queen Victoria to become the first woman in England to be delivered of a baby under chloroform – Prince Leopold in 1853.

Fifty-three children travelling third-class were drowned when the *Titanic* struck an iceberg and sank in the north Atlantic in 1912. All but one of the youngsters with first- or second-class accommodation escaped.

On 29 May 1453, Constantinople finally fell after a fierce and bloody fifty-three day siege to the Turkish sultan Mohammed II, who went on to capture Greece and to become absolute ruler of the vast Ottoman Empire.

Luxembourg City used to be surrounded by three rings of defence, including fifty-three forts linked by 16 miles (25·75 km) of tunnels and casemates hewn into solid rock.

The minimum weight of a standard-size egg is 53·2 g (1⅞ oz).

The winter of 1946/7 was the most severe in Britain for fifty-three years, but it was followed by one of the best summers since records have been kept.

54

The furthest distance away from a railway line in Great Britain is 54 miles (87 km) in the Highland region of Scotland.

A horse has fifty-four bones in its back.

A long term weather forecast from the Meteorological Office at Bracknell, Berkshire, covers a period of fifty-four days. A short term prediction is for only thirty-six hours.

The Orkneys are a group of fifty-four islands (twenty-eight inhabited) separated from the north of Scotland by the Pentland Strait.

Reg Harris, the world professional sprint cycling champion in the early 1950s, came out of retirement in 1974 and at fifty-four won the British professional 1,000-m title, beating men half his age!

By 1984 oil was being extracted from the North Sea at the rate of £54 million a day – £630 per second!

In 1846 fifty-four English retail cooperatives amalgamated to form the Cooperative Wholesale Society (now CRS), which today has over eleven million members.

Johnny Cockfield, an American boxer of recent years, won only two fights – he lost the other fifty-four!

An Hungarian mare called Kincsem set the as yet unbroken record of winning fifty-four consecutive races between 1876 and 1879.

The Royal yacht *Britannia* was launched at Clydebank, Scotland, in 1953, at a cost of nearly two million pounds. It replaced the fifty-four-year-old *Victoria and Albert* which was virtually unseaworthy.

55

The football pools companies usually give punters fifty-five matches to choose from.

Regular officers in the British armed forces are retired from the active list at the age of fifty-five.

The Isle of Man is 55 miles (88·5 km) from the coast of Lancashire.

Sir Douglas Bader, the 'tin-legged' air ace with twenty-two wartime 'kills' to his credit, and Kenneth More, his excellent impersonator in the popular film *Reach for the Sky*, died just fifty-five days apart in 1982.

Workers at Longbridge, Birmingham, produced on average a record fifty-five Austin Metros per man in 1983.

It is 55 miles (88 km) round the Isle of Wight, England's only self-contained county.

On 2 June 1982, Pope John Paul II was made the fifty-fifth freeman of the city of Cardiff.

The grey and red varieties found in British forests are just two of the fifty-five species of tree squirrels that live in Europe, Asia and America.

During 1947 snow fell in Britain every day from 22 January until 17 March – a total of fifty-five days.

Fifty-five million people – 20 million of them Russians – were killed during World War II.

56

About 56,000 people in Britain are off work every day with backache.

In the UK an average of 1,056 boys are born for every 1,000 girls, though their chance of survival is slightly less.

There were fifty-six revolutions in the Dominican Republic between 1844 and 1903.

Richard 'Beau' Nash (1674–1761) was for fifty-six years a celebrated master of ceremonies in Bath, which during the eighteenth century was among the most influential English cities. His eventual downfall was a compulsion for gambling.

Few people have borne stranger names than the man who masterminded the Japanese attack on Pearl Harbor in December 1941, Admiral Isoroku (Fifty-six) Yamamoto, whose father was that age when his latest child was born.

In the Middle Ages a holiday was truly a 'holy day'. There were fifty-six saints' days in England alone, when everybody was expected to attend church.

Fifty-six cameras were needed to film the spectacular scenes such as the epic chariot race in the 1959 film *Ben Hur*, starring Charlton Heston.

There are fifty-six ethnic groups in China.

The disgraced thirty-seventh US president Richard Nixon was featured a record fifty-six times on the cover of *Time* magazine over a twenty-five year period.

Of over two thousand lifeboat stations in Britain, fifty-six are operational all the year round.

57

The Scottish philanthropist Andrew Carnegie (1835–1919) received the freedom of fifty-seven cities.

Sunderland FC was in the First Division of the English Football League for a record fifty-seven consecutive seasons from 1890 until 1958, excluding the war years.

Soviet merchant shipping uses fifty-seven worldwide routes.

Mrs Ruth Kistler of Portland, Oregon, USA had fame thrust upon her when she gave birth to a daughter Suzan in October 1956, 129 days after her fifty-seventh birthday!

Fifty-seven species of land mammal are native to the British Isles.

There are an estimated 57 million revolvers and guns in private possession in the USA.

Fifty-seven (of 4,500) workmen lost their lives during the construction of the Forth railway bridge, north of Edinburgh, between 1882 and 1890.

For many years the American canned food firm of H. J. Heinz Co Ltd advertized their world-marketed products with the slogan '57 Varieties'.

C. P. Scott was editor of the *Manchester Guardian* for fifty-seven years from 1872 to 1929, which remains a record in British journalism.

If the world's population was evenly distributed, it would average fifty-seven people to every square mile (2·6 sq km).

58

The Channel Islands were occupied by German armed forces from 30 June 1940, until 9 May 1945 – a period of just over fifty-eight months.

The USA has fifty-eight plants on its endangered species list.

There are fifty-eight cities in the UK – forty-seven in England, six in Scotland, three in Wales and two in Northern Ireland.

Fifty-eight per cent of men have reached an advanced state of baldness by the age of fifty.

Fifty-eight per cent of a hen's egg is albumen – the white part; 32 per cent is yolk and 10 per cent is shell.

Haile Selassie was Emperor of Ethiopia for fifty-eight years until deposed by a military coup in 1974. On Christmas Day, 1984, the world's last remaining Emperor – Hirohito, Japan's 124th successive ruler – celebrated fifty-eight years on the throne.

The shortest woman in recorded history was the Dutch girl Pauline Musters, who when she died in 1895 aged seventeen was only 58 cm (23 in) tall.

The Queen's husband, Prince Philip, born on 10 June 1921, is fifty-eight months older than his wife.

Hydrofoils are in danger of disintegrating if they exceed a speed of 58 mph (93 kph).

In 1980 the Royal Mint of England produced coins for fifty-eight foreign countries.

59

King George III (1760–1820) reigned for over fifty-nine years and never once left England.

Richard Wagner (1813–83) laid the foundation stone of the Festival Theatre at Bayreuth, Bavaria, on his fifty-ninth birthday. Summer seasons of his operas – *Lohengrin*, *The Flying Dutchman*, etc. – have been given there in 1876, 1882–1944, and since 1951. A single seat would cost about £59!

Fifty-nine people, seven of them women, are entitled to append the prestigious letters RA (Royal Academician) after their names.

The French existentialist Jean-Paul Sartre (1905–80), declared the fifty-ninth winner of the Nobel prize for Literature in 1964, caused a sensation by refusing to accept the award.

John Ford's version of *Stagecoach* was the fifty-ninth film made by that genial Western hero John Wayne (1907–80). A classic of its genre, it made its star a household name.

Brighton finally won admission to the First Division in 1979 after fifty-nine years in the English Football League. They missed promotion the previous year on goal difference.

Each year over £20 million of prize money is won on Britain's fifty-nine horse-racing courses.

The hugely popular children's writer Enid Blyton (1898–1968) published fifty-nine of her 600 stories in 1955 alone!

The Republic of Texas was founded on 2 March 1836, by a group of fifty-nine Mexicans. It was admitted to the US in 1845 and remained the largest state until Alaska joined in 1959.

Parliament appointed 135 commissioners as judges to try Charles I (1600–49), but only seventy agreed to take part, and of these only fifty-nine actually signed the death warrant at Westminster Hall, London, on 27 January 1649. Three days later, a cold but brave king mounted the scaffold at Whitehall, and the Cromwellian era began.

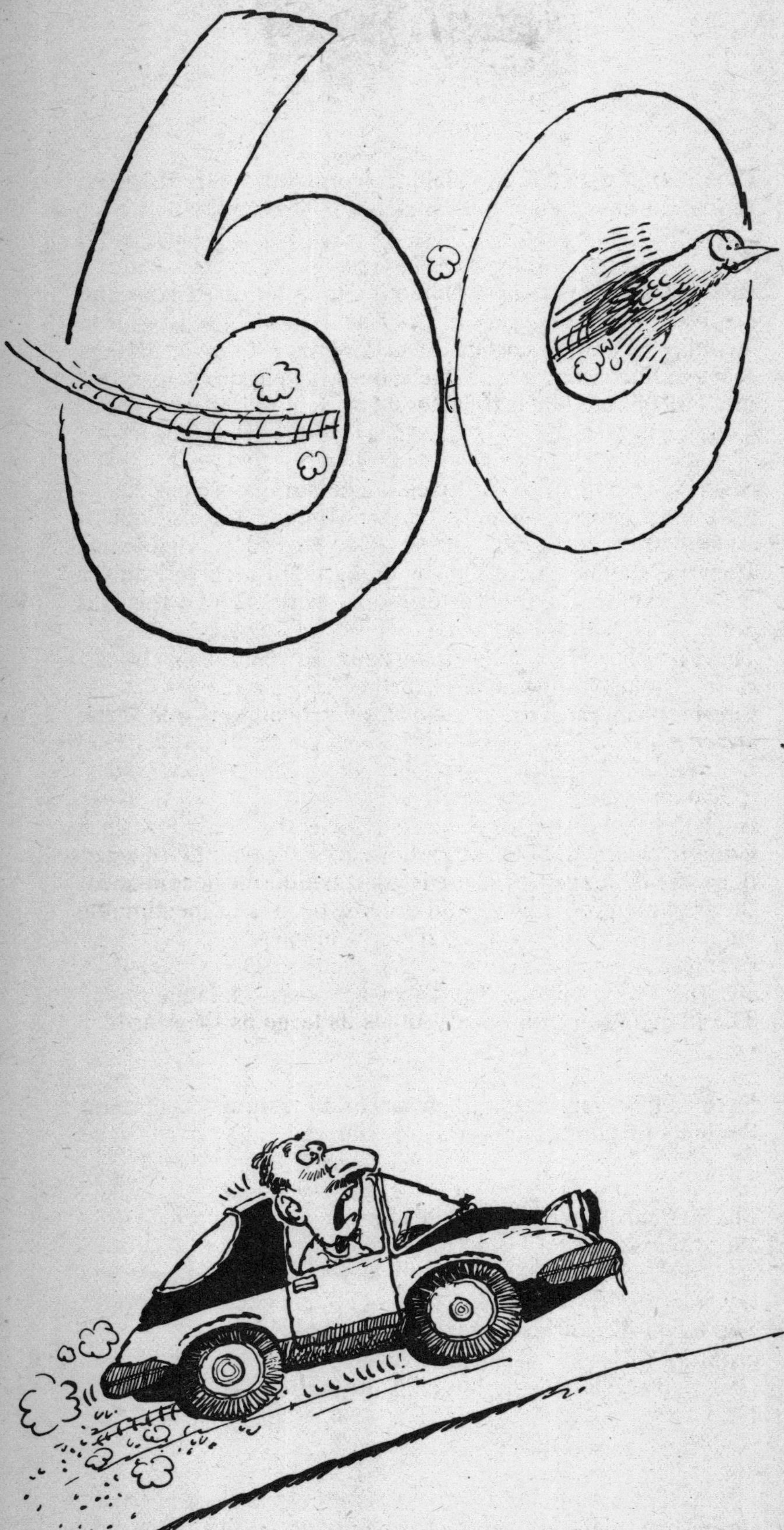

Pigeons can fly at 60 mph (96 kph).

60

Peter Minuit, the Dutch colonial governor from 1626–31, purchased what is now Manhattan Island from the Indian sachems for the derisory equivalent of 60 guilders ($24) worth of cloth and trinkets. The fruit of this modest speculation was the 'Big Apple' – modern New York City!

It is possible to circumnavigate the world without touching any land by keeping to latitude 60° S.

Sixty per cent of British foxes fail to survive a year.

England's 1966 World Cup winning team received only a basic £60 each for their afternoon's work. But to this was added a £1,000 bonus!

Condensed milk is made by evaporating 60 per cent of the water from fresh whole milk or skimmed milk. Gail Borden, an American, took out the first patent in 1856.

Cobalt 60 is a radioactive isotope of cobalt – the number denotes its atomic mass. It is used widely in hospitals for the treatment of cancer, and in industry it is of inestimable value in determining weak spots in metal.

The planet Neptune is sixty times as large as the Earth.

Every sixty minutes 520 buses pass through Trafalgar Square in London.

Pigeons can fly at 60 mph (96 kph).

During a good summer a colony of 60,000 bees can produce 24·5 kg (54 lb) of honey.

61

Baby alligators and pythons are born after sixty-one days.

One in every sixty-one people in the UK is called Smith – there are 900,000 of them!

The *Riesenrad* (Giant Wheel) in Vienna's amusement park, the Prater, is 61 m (197 ft) in diameter and has 120 spokes. Its height above ground is 64·75 m (209 ft). Marvellous views!

Mohammed Ali, the only man to regain the World Heavyweight Boxing Championship twice, had sixty-one professional fights between 1960 and 1981, which grossed over 50 million dollars.

On his final visit to Nazareth, where he had spent his childhood, Jesus went into the synagogue on the sabbath and read the first two verses from Chapter 61 of the Book of Isaiah.

Three of the most popular of all violin concertos were the sixty-first published works of their composers: Beethoven's in D (1806), Saint-Saens's No 3 in B minor (1881) and Elgar's in D (1906).

Mrs Florence Warboys of Ashwell, Hertfordshire, was Britain's oldest postwoman until her retirement in October 1983, after sixty-one years' service. A knee injury prevented her from riding her bicycle any longer!

Glasgow claims to have sixty-one swimming pools, an average of one for every 16,000 inhabitants.

The sixty-first recipient, in 1937, of the prestigious Order of Merit was Lord Baden Powell of Gilwell (1857–1941), who thirty years before had experimented with camps for boys, which led to the Boy Scout Association being granted a royal charter in 1912.

When Yorkshireman Geoffrey Boycott hit his twenty-first Test century in the sixth Test match against Australia at the Oval in 1981, he broke Colin Cowdrey's all-time record by making his sixty-first score of fifty or more runs in international cricket (forty 50s, twenty-one 100s).

62

The Roman poet and philosopher Cicero (106–43 BC) was sixty-two when he wrote *Reflections on Old Age* – it was one of the first and is still an authoritative study of a stage of life that everybody would wish to experience.

During World War II the Allies mobilized 62 million men and women.

The Public Records Office in Chancery Lane, London, needs 62 miles (100 km) of thick slate shelving to house all its documents, such as wills, and birth, marriage and death certificates.

The first sixty-two soldiers and sailors to be awarded the Victoria Cross – Britain's highest award for gallantry – received their medals from the proud sovereign herself in Hyde Park, London, on 26 June 1857.

Sixty-two per cent of Britons now travel abroad by air.

England's footballers have scored sixty-two 'hat-tricks' (three goals by one player) in international matches since 1872. The latest was by Luther Blissett (Watford) in the 10–0 defeat of Luxembourg in the European Cup competition in December 1981.

Menes, the first king of a united Egypt (*c* 3120–2890 BC), ruled for sixty-two years, and then had the misfortune to be killed by a hippopotamus, according to the priest Manetho, whose *History of Egypt* appeared around 300 BC.

Alligators have been known to live up to sixty-two years – about a dozen more than the Nile crocodile.

In 1919 it took sixty-two days for a military convoy to cross the USA from Washington DC to San Francisco – a distance of 2,500 miles (4,000 km). Today it is possible to do the same journey in sixty-two hours.

Large-size eggs weigh 62 g (2¼ oz) or more.

63

At the outbreak of World War I in 1914 Britain had only sixty-three serviceable military aircraft. France could muster 136 machines, Germany possessed 198 and Russia had 224.

Household names in the Principality, Gareth Edwards and J. P. R. Williams jointly hold the record of sixty-three appearances for Wales in Rugby Union internationals.

Fascinating research conducted in 1972 led to claims that 63 per cent of British homes contained at least one teddy bear!

Not even Martina Navratilova has eclipsed the Australian tennis ace Margaret Smith, who between 1960 and 1975 won a record sixty-three major tennis titles, among them ten Wimbledon and eighteen US championships.

Sixty-three bridges had to be constructed before the world's first public railway, linking Liverpool and Manchester, could be opened on 15 September 1830.

The 'Addled Parliament' of King James I lasted only sixty-three days from 5 April to 7 June 1614. During that time not a single measure passed into law.

A slice of white bread will provide sixty-three calories of energy.

To add a touch of realism, sixty-three lions were used in Mervyn Le Roy's epic film *Quo Vadis* (1951).

Modern astronomical calculations, supported by Biblical evidence, have led to the conclusion that the birth of Jesus took place on 23 October – sixty-three days before the traditional date – in the year 7 BC.

The world's population is increasing at the rate of 63 million people a year.

64

'Stardust', the best-selling song by Hoagy Carmichael, is sixty-four bars long, double the normally acceptable limit. The clarinettist Artie Shaw first made it a 'hit' in 1940, and it has remained popular every since.

For just sixty-four days England's Randolph Turpin (1928–66) was World Middleweight Boxing Champion. He became a national hero by outpointing Sugar Ray Robinson (USA) over fifteen rounds at Earl's Court, London, on 10 July 1951, but was stopped in the tenth round of a return contest in New York nine weeks later.

In the period 1963 to 1973 some sixty-four ships registered with Lloyd's of London just disappeared!

Louis Armstrong (1900–71), the genial black trumpeter with the gravelly voice, was sixty-four when he made his first million-selling record 'Hello Dolly' in 1964.

There are sixty-four London Transport bus garages in London.

Britain can claim sixty-four species of butterfly, thirty-seven of which may be spotted in Burnwood Forest, north of Oxford, at present under threat by a proposed extension of the M40 motorway.

The impressive memorial to Sir Walter Scott towers 61 m (200 ft) above Princes Street Gardens in Edinburgh. Niches contain statues of sixty-four characters from the great novelist's works.

The carbon content of peat, used as a fuel in Ireland and Denmark where there are no natural coal deposits, is as much as 64 per cent.

Moscow broadcasts to the world in sixty-four different languages.

Of the sixty-four pharaonic tombs discovered in the Valley of the Kings, near Luxor (ancient Thebes), the most exciting was that of the twenty-year-old Tutankhamun (reigned 1360–1350 BC), which was still rich in treasure and included a solid gold death mask and coffin. It was discovered by the English archaeologist Howard Carter and his patron Lord Carnarvon in 1922.

65

In the UK men aged sixty-five and over are entitled to an Old Age Pension. Worldwide it is recognized as a suitable retirement age, and the first US President George Washington (1732–99) set an early example.

Sixty-five so-called ‘frivolous parties’ were represented in the General Election of June 1983. Mrs Thatcher, whose Conservative government was returned to power, had eighteen fringe contenders in her Finchley seat.

British fresh pork sausages must by law have a meat content of at least 65 per cent.

Since its foundation in 1969, over 65,000 people pursuing 138 courses have obtained Open University degrees.

Heavy snow left a family marooned for sixty-five days on their isolated farm on Dartmoor from 23 December 1962 to the 2 March 1963 – virtually the whole of the winter!

Sixty-five per cent of British women go out to work.

Although only 2 per cent of Switzerland’s 6·3 million inhabitants are Germans, 65 per cent are German-speaking.

San Francisco Bay is 65 miles (104 km) long.

The coelacanth, a large black-grey fish 1·5 m (5 ft) in length, is generally described as a ‘living fossil’. Thought to have been extinct for 65 million years, one was caught off the coast of East Africa in 1938, and fishing boats have landed several since. They would appear to live in a reef close to the island of Madagascar.

Sixty-five per cent of the Earth’s crust is silica, which is a mineral formed by the natural bonding of silicon and oxygen, the two most abundant elements.

66

The longest book of prose in the Bible is the twenty-third – that of the prophet Isaiah. Its sixty-six chapters (1,290 verses) deal mainly with the fall of Judah.

Sixty-six fire brigades – all but five from London – fought the blaze which destroyed the Crystal Palace at Sydenham in 1936.

The Arctic and Antarctic Circles follow the lines of latitude 66½°N and 66½°S respectively.

Sixty-six spectators were crushed to death following a Rangers–Celtic match at Ibrox Park, Glasgow, in 1971, when a barrier collapsed as they made their way towards the exit down fateful stairway 13.

A record number of sixty-six horses competed in the 1929 Grand National steeplechase race at Aintree, near Liverpool.

Polymer 66 was the original name of nylon, invented in 1934. Nylon is an acronym of New York and London, where the artificial fibre was developed.

Sixty-six per cent – or two out of every three – British farmers own their land.

British people consume on average 66 kg (146 lb) of meat per head per annum – about twice as much as in 1860.

In constructing the remarkable Tokyo–Osaka New Tokaido Line, Japanese engineers had to bore sixty-six tunnels, the combined length of which (42 miles; 67·6 km) was equal to one-eighth the overall distance. Trains using the rail system reach speeds of over 130 mph (209 kph).

The diameter of the standard bicycle wheel is 66 cm (26 in).

67

During the weeks including Thanksgiving Day (the fourth Thursday in November) and Christmas Day, Americans consume 67 million turkeys!

In 1981 there were over 67,000 homeless families in Britain.

During February 1953, winds of up to 115 mph (185 kph) whipped up the North Sea sufficiently to tear sixty-seven major breaks in the dykes of western Holland.

Sixty-seven stories were printed in the British press about Prince Charles during his first term at a preparatory school in Cheam, Surrey, in 1955.

Rameses II, the Egyptian conqueror of the Hittites who died in his sixty-seventh year had four colossal 20·4 m (67 ft) seated likenesses of himself cut into the rock temple of Abu Simbel (*c* 1300 BC).

Sixty-seven sites were used in and around Los Angeles to stage the 1984 Olympic Games.

Sixty-seven out of every 100 loaves bought in Britain have been baked by the large bakery plants. No wonder mother is proud!

Adriana Martinez and Octavio Guillen, both aged eighty-two, finally married in Mexico City in June 1969, after an engagement of sixty-seven years!

Three English monarchs died at the age of sixty-seven. They were Henry I (1068–1135), after a reign of thirty-five years, George I (1660–1727), king for thirteen years, and George IV (1762–1830), who occupied the throne for a decade.

Ex-policeman Geoffrey Capes retired at the end of the 1980 athletics season after making a record sixty-seven appearances for England as a shot-putter. His UK record throw was 21·68 m (71 ft 1½ in). In 1984 he won, at the third attempt, the World's Strongest Man competition.

68

Abhorred for his cruelty and excesses, the tyrant Nero was finally condemned to death by the Roman senate. Lacking the courage to take his own life, he ordered a servant to kill him. His last words on 9 June AD 68 are said to have been: 'Ah, what an artist perishes with me . . .'

Guinea pigs are born after a sixty-eight day gestation period.

A Legal & General Insurance survey in 1983 established the outlay for the first sixteen years of a child's life to be £68,000!

The most countries ever represented in a Miss World Competition were sixty-eight in 1975.

The sixty-eight episodes of the Edwardian saga *Upstairs, Downstairs* were compulsive viewing for millions on Independent Television for five years from 1971.

There are sixty-eight police forces in the UK – thirty-seven in England, twenty in Scotland, five in Wales, one in Northern Ireland and five of a specialized nature.

The Mersey, on whose estuary stands Liverpool, is 68 miles (109 km) long. So too is the Towy, the longest river in Wales, which winds its way through the dairy farmlands of Dyfed.

Sixty-eight per cent of the cheese made in Britain is eaten by the British.

Since 1900 sixty-eight mammal species have become extinct.

A violin bow is 68·5 cm (27 in) long and contains about 150 horse hairs.

69

Sixty-nine per cent of British beef is now produced by crossing beef bulls with dairy cows.

At the outbreak of World War I in 1914, 69 per cent of Britain's wealth was controlled by just 1 per cent of the population.

The River Thames is tidal as far as Teddington Lock, Greater London, 69 miles (111 km) from the estuary mouth.

Ashley's British Factory Act of 1833 was undoubtedly a cause for wild rejoicing among teenagers of the day: it limited the hours of work to sixty-nine a week for young persons up to eighteen years of age.

Eleanor Farjeon (1881–1965) wrote sixty-nine highly praised books for children, all characterized by magic, humour and vivacity, and to be found in most libraries.

The first wife of Fyodor Vassilet, a Russian peasant from near Moscow, had twenty-seven confinements which produced sixty-nine children (twenty sets of twins, seven of triplets and four of quads). She died aged fifty-six, and her husband was desolated without her.

On only sixty-nine occasions has a bowler taken all ten wickets in a cricket innings. A. P. Freeman of Kent managed it in 1929, 1930 and 1931.

The Federal District of Columbia (DC), which contains the US capital Washington, covers an area of 69 sq miles (172 sq km).

Under the management of Sir Alf Ramsey, England's soccer team played 113 games between 1962 and 1973 and won sixty-nine of them. They drew twenty-seven and lost seventeen. In 1966 England won the World Cup at Wembley.

Sixty-nine million Penny Black postage stamps were issued in Britain from 1840. One in excellent condition would today be worth £2,500!

The Australian Jack Gregory scored the fastest ever cricket Test century – in just seventy minutes – against South Africa at Johannesburg during the tour of 1920–21.

70

Said to be over a thousand years old, Cowthorpe Oak, near Wetherby, West Yorkshire, will hold seventy people in its hollow.

The Australian Jack Gregory scored the fastest ever cricket Test century – in just seventy minutes – against South Africa at Johannesburg during the tour of 1920–21.

Cancer victim Ian Fleming (1909–64) – the creator of secret agent 007 James Bond – smoked seventy hand-made cigarettes a day.

The kernel of the mature coconut contains 70 per cent oil.

In the reign of William the Conqueror (1066–87) there were seventy mints in England issuing coins of the realm.

It is possible to travel the breadth of Canada from Montreal across the Rocky Mountains to Vancouver, or vice versa, a distance of 2,918 miles (4,695 km), in seventy hours by the Canadian Pacific Railway, opened in 1885.

Alexander the Great (356–323 BC), the brilliant Macedonian general, is credited with founding seventy towns or cities, the most renowned being, of course, Alexandria in Egypt (331 BC). He named another, Thessalonika in northern Greece, after his sister.

It might come as a surprise to many British motorists, but 70 mph (113 kph) is actually the legal speed limit on all motorways throughout the nation.

It took seventy years to produce the Oxford English Dictionary, and the first edition was published in 1929.

Only 70 boys actually live in Eton College. They are the King's Scholars and Oppidans. The other students live in houses supervised by the masters.

71

Pink Panther, the cartoon creation of David de Patie and Fritz Freberg, featured in seventy-one films between 1964 and 1972.

The maximum circumference of a soccer football of international quality is 71 cm (28 in).

Neil Kinnock (born 1942) won the leadership of the Labour Party on 2 October 1983, with a vote of 71·272 per cent in a four-cornered contest at Brighton.

Charlie Chaplin (1889–1977) initially established his reputation in seventy-one short slapstick comedies made between 1914 and 1923 by Mack Sennett.

Stegosaurus, a 6·6 tonne (6½ ton) dinosaur covered with bony plates like armour, had a feeble brain weighing only 71 g (2½ oz).

The great 'Brown Bomber', Joe Louis (1914–81), who held the World Heavyweight Boxing Championship from 1937 until 1949, had seventy-one fights, of which he lost only three. He defended his title a record twenty-five times, and only four of his opponents lasted the distance!

Scotland is represented at Westminster by seventy-one Members of Parliament.

The Apache chief Geronimo (1829–1908), who had fought bravely, often against immense odds, to prevent white domination of south-west America, was finally captured at Skeleton Canyon in Arizona in 1886 along with seventy followers. Most of them died without regaining their freedom, and the surviving few were not released until 1914.

The world's fastest jet plane currently in service is the American Lockheed SR-71. It is made of titanium in order to withstand the immense heat generated by flying at speeds up to 2,200 mph (3,540 kph).

The world's coldest township is Oymyakon in Siberia, where in 1964 a temperature of −71°C (−96°F) was recorded.

72

There are seventy-two local radio stations in the UK.

72 miles (115·8 km) of the original 120 miles (193 km) of the Pilgrim's Way, a route from Winchester to Canterbury, still survive.

The normal pulse rate for an adult human is seventy-two beats per minute.

The longest running show in the seventy-two year history of the world-famous London Palladium was the musical *Barnum*, which ran from June 1980 to February 1983, and starred the lively Michael Crawford.

Aeschylus (525–456 BC) has been described as 'the father of the Greek drama'; only seven of his seventy-two plays survive today.

There are seventy-two counties in the UK – forty-six in England, nine mainland and three island territories in Scotland, eight in Wales and six in Northern Ireland.

Seventy-two per cent of National Health Service prescriptions are free.

The Ugly Duckling was the last of Walt Disney's seventy-two Silly Symphonies, produced between 1929 and 1939.

The Septuagint, a Greek version of the combined Old Testament and Apocrypha, is said to have been the work of seventy-two Palestinian Jews (six scholars from each of the twelve tribes) completed on Pharos Island in seventy-two days at the command of Ptolemy Philadelphus (308–246 BC.

The army career of Joseph Wenzel, Count Radetsky von Radetz, (1766–1858) spanned seventy-two years. He was made a Field Marshal in 1836. Twelve years later, at the age of eighty-two he came out of semi-retirement to lead the Austrians to victory over the Italians at Novara in March 1849. A famous march by Johann Strauss is dedicated to this unusual soldier and national hero.

73

Said by her proud builders to be sure to last a millenium, Brighton's old Chain Pier was destroyed during a violent storm only seventy-three years after construction was completed in 1823.

There are seventy-three corners in the 14·2 mile (22·85 km) death-defying circuit of the Nurburgring, scene of the German Grand Prix motor racing event.

Seventy-three saints are commemorated in the Calendar of the Book of Common Prayer.

Leon Trotsky (1879–1940), who lost out in a power struggle with Joseph Stalin after Lenin's death in 1924, survived an assassination attempt by Soviet agents, who sprayed the bedroom of his home in Coyoacan, Mexico City, with seventy-three bullets! He was fatally wounded with an ice pick four months later by a Spanish communist, Ramon Mercader.

Elvis Presley's discs headed the British Hit Parade for a record total of seventy-three weeks.

Saint Benedict (*c* AD 480–547) set out his famous *Rule* in seventy-three short chapters which outline the principles of Western monasticism.

Seventy-three airline companies from sixty-eight countries operate scheduled services into Heathrow Airport, London.

When the Beatles appeared on the popular Ed Sullivan Show during their first US tour in 1964, they were watched by 73 million viewers.

Lapland, which spreads across the northern parts of Norway, Sweden, Finland and the Soviet Union, has two months of total darkness relieved only by a pale moon and the ghostly aurora borealis (northern lights). This is followed by seventy-three consecutive days of daylight!

Birmingham's water supply comes from Wales, 73 miles (117 km) away.

74

BL, formerly British Leyland, has a work-force of about 74,000 people.

The administration of Britain's prisons is in the hands of seventy-four governors.

The eleven Confederate states lost over 74,000 men in battle during the American Civil War of 1861–65.

The American actor Henry Fonda (1905–82) made seventy-four films between *The Farmer takes a Wife* in 1935 and *Midway* in 1976. His performances in *Young Mr Lincoln* (1939) and *The Grapes of Wrath* (1940) were especially memorable, and made him a household name. His children Jane and Peter have also had impressive screen careers.

The Gospel according to St Matthew was written in AD 74. Before becoming one of Christ's disciples, he was known as Levi, and he served Herod Antipas as a tax collector.

The Federal Republic of Germany – West Germany – is the seventy-fourth largest country in the world (95,815 sq miles; 248,161 sq km). Since 1949 the capital has been Bonn, the birthplace of Ludwig van Beethoven.

The Shops Act of 1912 made it compulsory for shops to close at 1 p.m. on at least one day a week. It also restricted the weekly working hours for assistants under eighteen to seventy-four including meal times. The forty-hour week was still a long term dream.

There are over 74,000 war widows in the UK.

In 1982 tax accounted for 74 per cent of the price of a packet of twenty cigarettes sold in Britain.

A Californian rancher called Martin Jaureguy claimed the equivalent of £45,000 from the US army for the loss of seventy-four of his cattle, machine-gunned by trigger-happy troopers when the cows stampeded during the uproar caused by manoeuvres.

75

The peak day in the Battle of Britain was 15th August 1940, when the RAF shot down seventy-five German planes for the loss of thirty-four of their own.

Seventy-five per cent of fathers are present at the birth of their children.

Seventy-five varieties of onions are grown commercially in Britain. Incidentally, all onions become sweet when cooked.

Only seventy-five troops formed the British garrison in the Falkland Islands before the Argentinian invasion of 1982.

Seventy-five per cent of all pig food consists of barley mixed with proteins and minerals.

As every winter sports enthusiast will know, a downhill slalom has a maximum of seventy-five gates for men and sixty for women.

Berlin is only 75 miles (120 km) from the West German border.

It is estimated that one in every seventy-five people in Britain is waiting for an operation.

The nine principal Channel Islands – Jersey, Guernsey, Alderney, Brechou, Great Sark, Little Sark, Herm, Jethou and Lihou – have a combined area of 75 sq miles (194 sq km), and have belonged to the British Crown since 1066.

Of 75,000 animals kept in quarantine since 1970, only one has developed rabies.

76

Seventy-six of the Sexton Blake books were written by Edwy Searles Brooks (note the S.B.). The fictional detective, a rival to Sherlock Holmes in popularity, first appeared in *The Missing Millionaire* in December 1893.

St Paul was among seventy-six people caught in a storm while sailing to Italy in AD 59. After drifting for a fortnight, they were finally shipwrecked off the coast of Malta, where they were kindly received by the inhabitants.

A Belgian cyclist called Leon Vanderstuyft covered just over 76 miles (122 km) in an hour at the Montlhery Motor Circuit, France, on 30 September 1928.

The Grenadier Guards, raised by the future King Charles II in 1656 while in exile in Bruges, have a record of seventy-six battle honours, including Waterloo, after which they adopted their present name and the bearskins worn by the defeated Grenadiers of Napoleon.

The life expectancy for British women is seventy-six, an increase of two years in the last decade.

Seventy-six per cent of Greater London's population would be dead within twelve weeks of a nuclear bomb attack.

A classic suit made by a Savile Row tailor requires seventy-six different pattern pieces.

The entire musical output of both Franz Liszt and Peter Ilyich Tchaïkovsky could be condensed to seventy-six hours playing time for each composer.

The greatest range ever achieved with an orthodox gun during the two world wars was 76 miles (122 km) by the 'Kaiser Wilhelm geschutz', sometimes mistakenly called 'Big Bertha', which shelled Paris in March 1918, killing 256 people.

There are only seventy-six indoor tennis courts in the whole of Great Britain. There are as many as this in the city of Paris alone. Advantage France!

77

The UK lost seventy-seven submarines during World War II.

Renowned for his fearsome punching power, Welshman Jimmy Wilde was World Flyweight Boxing Champion from 1916 until 1923. He won an unequalled seventy-seven of his 126 fights by knock-outs!

A British housewife averages a seventy-seven hour working week.

Sir John Mills made seventy-seven major films between *The Midshipman* (1932) and *The Water Babies* (1977), and won an Academy Award for his sterling performance in *Ryan's Daughter* (1971). His own daughters, Juliet and Hayley, have also enjoyed careers in movies.

In 1960 the US submarine *Triton* made a 36,014 mile (57,917 km) circumnavigation of the world, never once surfacing in a voyage of seventy-seven days.

Seventy-seven per cent of all dental caries occur in the molars – the back teeth used for chewing.

The Hampshire seaport of Southampton is 77 miles (124 km) south-west of London by rail.

Seventy-seven per cent of British executives use cars provided by their companies.

Mike Hailwood (1940–80) scored a total of seventy-seven championship event wins in motor-cycling, and won nine world titles between 1961 and 1967. He was fatally injured in a car accident.

One of New York's most distinctive skyscrapers is the needle-pointed Chrysler Building, and named after an American industrialist and car manufacturer. Completed in 1929, it has seventy-seven storeys and stands at a height of 320 m (1,048 ft).

'78

The boiling point of alcohol is 78·3°C (173°F).

The greatest number of catches taken in a cricket season, other than by a wicket-keeper, is seventy-eight by Walter Hammond (Gloucestershire) in 1928.

At peak times there are seventy-eight landings and take-offs every hour at Heathrow, London's busiest airport.

A human has seventy-eight back muscles. Ouch!

At the age of seventy-eight the seventh US president, Andrew Jackson (1829–37), became the first holder of the office to be officially photographed.

British Airways operates services to 150 cities in seventy-eight countries. The company uses 181 aircraft, notably twenty-five Boeing 747s, fifty-two Tridents and five Concordes.

Prior to the introduction of long play microgroove, most gramophone records played at or around 78 revolutions per minute and were made of a brittle substance called shellac. EMI discontinued their sale from 18 March 1959, but they are still widely collected by enthusiasts.

Seventy-eight per cent of the British population live in cities.

The remarkable American naive painter Grandma Moses (Anna Mary Robertson) was seventy-eight when she completed her very first canvas. By her death in 1961 aged 101, this arthritic ex-farm worker had produced over 1,500 oil paintings.

Experts estimate that 78,232 tonne (77,000 ton) of gold have been mined in the world. Enough gold has been produced in the last 500 years to make a cube measuring more than 14·9 m (49 ft) on each side.

'79

According to some intriguing research conducted by Dr Joyce Brothers, the average American woman kisses seventy-nine men before marriage!

An astonishing 79 per cent of the inhabitants of Calcutta, India's largest city with a population of 6½ million, are accommodated in one-room homes.

Nell Gwynn, ex-orange-seller and auburn-haired favourite of Charles II, lived from 1671 until her death in 1687 at No 79 Pall Mall, at the time London's most fashionable street.

The seventy-nine episodes of *Star Trek*, first screened on US television in 1966, had reached 131 overseas networks by 1983.

When the seventy-nine year-old Cardinal Stefan Wyzynski died on 28 May 1981, the bells of all seventy-nine of Warsaw's Catholic churches tolled in mourning for the revered Polish primate.

Seventy-nine per cent of a potato is water; only 16 per cent is starch.

Nazi Germany began the invasion of the Soviet Union – code name 'Barbarossa' – on 22 June 1941 with seventy-nine divisions of troops and armour.

The atomic number of gold or aurum (Au) is 79. This soft, ductile yellow element, which never dulls or corrodes, was first discovered and used at least 5,000 years ago.

The American pilot Charles Lindbergh (1902–74) was the seventy-ninth man to make a transatlantic flight, but the first to do so solo. He piloted his Ryan monoplane *The Spirit of St Louis* from Long Island, New York, to Le Bourget, Paris, completing the 3,610 miles (5,810 km) journey in thirty-three hours thirty minutes during 20/21 May 1927, and winning a prize of 25,000 dollars.

Seventy-nine transmitters (forty-seven of them in the UK and the remainder at relaying stations abroad) enable the BBC to broadcast 700 hours of programmes a week in thirty-seven languages.

There are eighty flushing toilets for dogs in Paris.

80

There are eighty flushing toilets for dogs in Paris.

Some 80 acres (11·2 hectares) of precious land – 17·6 per cent of the principality – have been reclaimed from the sea in recent years by land-starved Monaco. Incidentally, the Monegasque army consists of just eighty souls!

A suitable fuel for modern cars must have an octane rating in excess of eighty to overcome knocking.

In 1730 the French scientist René Réaumar (1683–1757) invented an alcohol thermometer with a graduated scale 0° freezing point and 80° boiling point. It had a long vogue in Scandinavia.

Agatha Christie's *The Mousetrap*, running in the West End, London, since 1952, was originally a radio play commissioned by the BBC to mark the eightieth birthday of the late Queen Mary.

The city of Birmingham has an area of 80·6 sq miles (208·8 sq km).

Cardinals must now retire when they reach the age of eighty.

Typing sixty words a minute uses up 80 calories of energy in an hour.

France's highest civil award, the Grand Cross of the Legion of Honour, instituted by Napoleon, is limited to eighty holders.

Eighty per cent of Britain's dairy herd are bred by artificial insemination.

81

Of American women who work only 19 per cent do so out of choice, the other 81 per cent must work because their families depend upon their income.

The eighty-first and last of the stable chemical elements was discovered in 1925 and named rhenium.

During a rodent extermination campaign launched during the winter of 1941–42 in the area around the Port of London, 81 per cent of those caught were black rats – the ones responsible for the Black Death in the Middle Ages and the Great Plague of 1665.

Forty-eight hours before the outbreak of World War II in September 1939, over 1¼ million women and children were evacuated from eighty-one nationwide pick-up points to stay in the country with strangers who had offered accommodation.

Mike Gibson scored a record eighty-first cap (sixty-nine for Ireland and twelve for Britain) when Ireland defeated Australia 9–3 at Brisbane on 17 June 1979.

The Swiss tenor Hugues Cuenod was eighty-one when he sang the Emperor in the première of the original version of Puccini's opera *Turandot* at the Barbican Centre, London, in November 1982!

Wyatt Earp died on 13 January 1929, at the age of eighty-one. As a marshal of Tombstone, Arizona, he had been the best known lawman in the American West. With his brother and 'Doc' Halloday, he triumphed in the epic gun fight against sheriff John Behan and a cowboy gang at the OK Corral in 1881.

Private transport accounts for 81 per cent of motorized passenger movement in Great Britain.

Britain has no less than 81,000 public houses.

81 per cent of the southern hemisphere is water and only 19 per cent is land.

82

There are only eighty-two men for every 100 women in the US capital, Washington DC.

Acting is a notoriously hazardous profession, and at any one time 82 per cent of the membership of Equity, the actors' union, are 'resting' – otherwise unemployed!

Married in 1883, James Frederick Burgess (1861–1966) and his wife Sarah Ann (1866–1965) were still together eighty-two years later – a British record.

The American Erle Stanley Gardner (1889–1970) wrote eighty-two Perry Mason adventures. Raymond Burr played the private investigator in a television series from 1957 to 1966.

There are 82 million households in the USA.

In 1952 the 54,173 tonne (53,320 ton) liner *United States* gained the Blue Riband for crossing the Atlantic in a record three days, ten hours (eighty-two hours) at an average speed of 33·5 knots.

British Telecom uses eighty-two directories to cover the entire UK.

Charles II died in February 1685, and his brother the Duke of York succeeded him as James II. The Duke of Monmouth, illegitimate son of Charles II and Lucy Walters, claimed the British throne, and with eighty-two followers landed at Lyme Regis, Dorset, in June, but was unable to rally the gentry to his cause. Badly defeated at Sedgemoor, Somerset, he fled but was soon captured. He was tried as a traitor and usurper, found guilty and beheaded.

Eighty-two thousand people filled Wembley Stadium when John Paul II held an open-air mass on 29 May 1982, during the first ever papal visit to Britain.

A horse can walk 82 m (90 yd) in a minute.

83

The Post Office service has a national network of eighty-three mechanical high speed sorting offices.

Ferenc Puskas owned, perhaps, the deadliest left foot shot in football. He proved the point by scoring eighty-three goals in eighty-four internationals for Hungary prior to the 1956 uprising.

Eighty-three miles (133·6 km) of sewers drain the 100 sq miles (259 sq km) of the City of London.

A distance of 83 miles (133·6 km) separates England's two tallest church buildings – St Paul's Cathedral, London (111 m; 365 ft) and Salisbury Cathedral, Wiltshire (123 m; 404 ft).

A promoter's nightmare occurred on 27 February 1951, at the Harringay Arena, London, when Don Cockell knocked out American Lloyd Marshall in thirty-five seconds and Randolph Turpin demolished Belgium's Luc Van Dam in forty-eight seconds – a total of just eighty-three seconds for the two big money boxing events!

In 1981 over 83,000 people – more than half of them men – were prosecuted for shop-lifting in the UK.

The taciturn Gary Cooper (1901–61) made eighty-three major films between *It* (1927) and *The Naked Edge* (1961). His death from cancer was mourned by millions worldwide.

A work of immense fascination, though scarcely known to the general public, is the Overlord Embroidery, completed in 1973 after five years' effort. It is a modern equivalent of the renowned Bayeaux Tapestry. It is 83 m (272 ft) long and 1 m (3·2 ft) wide; and it depicts in thirty-four detailed sections the part played by Britain in World War II.

The Pope is protected in Vatican City State by the oldest regular army in the world – the eighty-three strong Swiss Guard, founded in January 1506.

When Miss Sheila Chisholm, flying a single engine Cessna Centurion, arrived in Australia from Britain on 22 November 1980, she had established a new record for a solo flight between the two countries of eighty-three hours.

84

Greater London is represented in Parliament by eighty-four MPs.

84 Charing Cross Road was a best seller for the New York writer Helene Hanff. It was based on a unique twenty year correspondence with Frank Doel, the chief buyer for an impeccable London bookshop, and it has been turned into a film.

One in every eighty-four pregnancies results in twins.

The Belgian novelist Georges Simenon (born 1903) wrote his eighty-fourth and final novel featuring his detective creation Inspector Maigret in 1972.

Among the events at the opening ceremony of the 1984 Olympic Games in Los Angeles was the spectacular sight of eighty-four grand pianos – complete with white-tailed pianists – playing a Gershwin tune to evoke the vintage years of Hollywood.

Discipline in the British Army used to be terribly harsh. For example, Private John Wilson of the 84th Yorkshire and Lancashire Regiment was court-martialled at Bangalore, India, in 1815 – the year of Waterloo – for refusing to accept the daily rum ration! His claim that he had refrained from drink all his life failed to save him from the firing squad.

If a person drives to Italy by way of the famous Brenner Pass, opened in the eighteenth century, he or she has to negotiate no less than eighty-four curves in the twisty road.

Eighty-four per cent of Britain's wealth is owned by 7 per cent of the population.

An estimated 84 million people play bridge, a card game of much skill which acquired its name from two English couples who had to cross Istanbul's famous Galata Bridge every time they met for a game in each other's home.

Navvies employed on the construction of Britain's railway network between 1830 and 1850 worked twelve hours every day, making a total of eighty-four hours a week. For this tremendous effort they were each paid the princely sum of £1!

85

With an automatic milking machine called a rotating carousel, a British dairy farmer can now milk eighty-five cows in an hour.

Spain accounts for 85 per cent of the Iberian peninsula

About 85 per cent of people have blood containing the rhesus factor, and are known as rhesus positive (R+); the others are rhesus negative (R−). It is important in blood transfusions not to mix the two.

When the last Germans withdrew from Poland's capital Warsaw on 16 January 1945, 800,000 people had died and 85 per cent of the city lay devastated.

In 1239 the Hanseatic League was established between certain north German cities for their mutual prosperity and protection. At its peak there were eighty-five members, notably Hamburg, Lubeck and Bremen.

Wrangler jeans, a product of the US firm Blue Bell Incorporated, are marketed in eighty-five countries and manufactured in seventeen.

The eighty-fifth birthday celebrations in 1966 of the prolific Spanish painter Pablo Picasso (1881–1973) did full justice to his enormous reputation. They included an exhibition of 1,000 of his works at three galleries in Paris, insured for $60 million.

Billy Wright (born 1924), a brilliant centre half, captained England's soccer team eighty-five times. He won 105 caps, and in so doing became the first ever player to pass the century mark.

Frequent exposure to sounds above 85 decibels can often result in an incurable loss of hearing. A music centre with the volume turned right up will register around 100 decibels!

The Universata Esperanto Asocio, founded in 1908, has members in eighty-five countries. Esperanto is an international language invented by the Pole Ludovic Zamenhof (1859–1917). It can be learned in a fifth of the time normally required to master a new tongue.

86

There are eighty-six zoos and safari parks in the UK.

The popular American television series *Dallas* had been screened in eighty-six countries by the beginning of 1984.

The Salvation Army, founded by William Booth in 1878, operates in eighty-six countries throughout the world.

The Empire State Building, erected by 1931, was originally designed to be eighty-six storeys high (335 m; 1,100 ft). However, the 'completed' structure failed to satisfy the aesthetic taste of the builders, who added a further sixteen floors (45·7 m; 150 ft).

Suzuki, Yamaha, Honda and Kawasaki. When was the last time you saw a British made motor bike? By 1979 eighty-six out of every 100 motor-cycles registered in the UK were of Japanese origin.

The lowest point in the USA is Death Valley, California, which is 86 m (282 ft) below sea level and subject to temperatures of up to 60°C (140°F).

Eighty-six deliveries were all England's Ian Botham needed to score a century against Australia in the fifth Test at Old Trafford, Manchester, in August 1981, the least since 1902, when Gilbert Jessop slammed a hundred off seventy-five balls against the Australian tourists.

The Italian astronomer Giovanni Cassini (1625–1712) estimated the distance between the Earth and the Sun as 86 million miles (138 million km) – not a bad guess for those days. The mean average is in fact an extra 7 million miles (12 million km).

The Class 86 locomotives used on the overhead electrified system of British Rail serving London, Birmingham, Liverpool and Manchester can reach a speed of 100 mph (161 kph).

The sturdy St Bernard dog, used for guiding and mountain rescue in Switzerland, stands an impressive 86 cm (34 in) at the shoulders.

87

Eighty-seven per cent of cows' milk is water.

Joe Davis (1901–78) – the 'king of pot' – made eighty-seven breaks of over 1,000 at billiards and 687 centuries at snooker, including the first ever maximum of 147 in competitive play in 1955.

The Heathrow extension of London Transport's Piccadilly line required a new fleet of eighty-seven six-car trains, which entered service in July 1975. They are 1·8 m (6 ft) longer than normal to accommodate extra luggage.

You might not believe it but the Post Office insists that over 87 per cent of first-class mail arrives the day after it has been sent.

In the early days of World War II, when Germany's aircraft outnumbered Britain's by 3 to 1, an RAF pilot's expectation of life was not more than eighty-seven flying hours!

Eighty-seven per cent of the white of an egg – the albumen – is water. Only 12 per cent is protein and 1 per cent is mineral.

Eighty-seven per cent of British people aged over seventy-five have lost all their teeth.

In 1969, when safety measures were less sophisticated than they are today, forty aircraft in the USA alone and forty-seven elsewhere fell victim to hi-jackers.

By 1970, the year of its Diamond Jubilee, there were eighty-seven member countries of the World Association of Girl Guides and Girl Scouts. Fifty were full members and thirty-seven were associate members.

Australian cricketers dislike reaching a score of eighty-seven runs. As it is only thirteen short of a century, it is regarded as being an unlucky number. One more run and the tension visibly eases from a batsman's face!

88

In 1981 HM Customs foiled attempts to smuggle into Britain a total of eighty-eight cats and dogs.

For eighty-eight days in the winter of 1962/3 Leonardo da Vinci's 'Mona Lisa' was exhibited in Washington and New York at the instigation of President John F. Kennedy.

Eighty-eight per cent of the population of Pakistan are Moslems.

London Transport's One Man Operated (OMO) buses hold eighty-eight passengers: forty-four seated upstairs, twenty-four on the lower deck, and twenty standing.

In 88 BC the vengeful Jewish high priest Jannaeus had several hundred of his own people crucified before him on a hill outside Jerusalem as a punishment for rebellion.

Brian Boru (born AD 926), King of All-Ireland from 1001 to 1014, was eighty-eight when he won his final battle at Clontarf. He was killed in his command tent by fleeing Vikings.

Some eighty-eight communities in Austria still wear national dress on special occasions.

The most glamorous wrestler in the years just after World War II was Gorgeous George, who had eighty-eight satin costumes, ermine jock-straps and a tail-coated valet. The latter led the wrestling hero to and from the ring, bearing on a silver tray a monogrammed towel, a prayer rug and various spray guns.

In 1665, the Great Plague reached the Derbyshire village of Eyam, whose rector prevailed upon the inhabitants to isolate themselves to prevent the disease spreading elsewhere. A year later, all but eighty-eight of the community of 350 had died. One woman lost her husband and six children within a week.

One of the most effective German weapons of World War II was a field gun measuring only 88 mm (3½ in).

89

A refrigerator can now be found in 89 per cent of British homes.

A hamburger bun provides 89 calories of energy.

The lowest number of days in three consecutive months is eighty-nine – February (twenty-eight), March (thirty-one) and April (thirty).

The gestation period for an Indian elephant is eighty-nine weeks.

There are eighty-nine laws in the UK which make it an offence to disclose information without permission.

The 89th Military Airlift Wing of the US Air Force has at its disposal twenty-three aircraft to transport important government officials on about 1,000 flights a year.

Winter is officially eighty-nine days long: from 22 December to 20 March.

Jupiter's equatorial diameter is 89,000 miles (143,000 km) – noticeably larger than its polar diameter of 84,000 miles (135,000 km).

Earl Clement Attlee (1883–1967), Churchill's wartime deputy and British Prime Minister from 1945 to 1951, became the eighty-ninth person to receive the Order of Merit (1955). He was Leader of the Socialist Party from 1935 until his retirement.

Bournes, formerly Bournes and Hollingsworth, of Oxford Street, London – once renowned for the sale of school uniforms – closed down in 1983 after eighty-nine years of trading.

90

It took ninety years for England's soccer team to be beaten by a foreign side at home – Hungary beat them 6–3 at Wembley on 25 November 1953.

90

A bull terrier – fearsome beast! – once killed 500 rats in ninety minutes.

The average British family now uses ninety rolls of toilet tissue (about 2 miles; 3·2 km) every year.

Heavy lorries – juggernauts – are said to cause 90 per cent of the damage to road surfaces in Britain.

A Belgian idiosyncrasy of the French language is to say and write *septante* instead of *soixante-dix* (seventy) and *nonante* instead of *quatre-vingt-dix* (ninety).

Cuba is only 90 miles (145 km) south of Key West, Florida, the southern tip of the USA.

Mount Everest (8,848 m; 29,028 ft) is over ninety times higher than the highest point in Holland (98 m; 321 ft).

The blue whale and killer whale each have a life span of about ninety years.

The aurora borealis or northern lights – bright, luminous beams seen in the night sky in northern latitudes – are visible in many parts of Britain north of the Wash, and on average ninety times a year in the Orkneys.

It took ninety years for England's soccer team to be beaten by a foreign side at home – Hungary beat them 6–3 at Wembley on 25 November 1953.

The temperature on the moon at midday is about 90°C (195°F) at its equator. At night it falls dramatically to −130°C (−200°F).

91

The world's longest single span suspension bridge is the £91 million Humber Bridge which was officially opened by the Queen on 17 July 1981. Over 1 mile (1·6 km) long, it links Hull with the south bank of the River Humber.

In 1967, when he was ninety-one the Welsh composer Havergal Brian wrote three symphonies, Nos 30–32.

Sovereigns and guineas, long out of circulation but still collectors' pieces, were made of 91·66 per cent pure gold, the rest of the metal being copper.

The numbers 1 to 13 add up to 91.

The hulk of the *Mary Rose*, the pride of Henry VIII's navy, which sank in stormy weather in the English Channel in 1545, was successfully raised from the seabed in late 1982. Its original armament had included ninety-one guns, the heaviest being positioned in innovatory fashion between decks.

The smallest obtuse angle is 91°.

Ninety-one countries require vaccination against smallpox: twenty-seven African; twenty-six American; twenty-two Asian; fourteen European; and two Australasian.

There have been ninety-one individual scores in cricket of 300 or more runs in an innings. Only eleven of these were in Test matches, the highest being 365 not out by Gary Sobers for West Indies against Pakistan at Kingston, Jamaica, in the 1957–58 season.

Runways are usually 91 m (100 yd) wide and up to 2 miles (3·2 km) long.

There are ninety-one vehicles for every mile (1·6 km) of road in Britain.

92

Ninety-two per cent of the football pools market in the UK is controlled by just two companies, Littlewoods and Vernons, both with headquarters in Liverpool.

Anthracite, a black coal with a brilliant lustre, contains 92 per cent or more of carbon and will burn steadily without any noxious smoke or flame.

Olympic Gold medals are actually 92 per cent silver – the rest is gilt.

Summer, as far as the Meteorological Office is concerned, consists of the ninety-two days from 1 June to 31 August.

Belgian crime novelist George Simenon, author of over 500 books, could type ninety-two words in a minute.

Ninety-two per cent of British telephone subscribers can now dial direct to ninety-two countries.

The National Health Service provides medical care for 92 per cent of the British population.

Ninety-two per cent of the work-force in nursing are women.

Ninety-two European magazines, as well as sixteen American, carried cover pictures of Raquel Welch following her sensational appearance in the 1966 movie *One Million Years BC*. Instant fame!

It takes only ninety-two minutes to travel by Inter City Express train from Euston, London, to Birmingham, England's second largest city.

93

Ninety-three out of every 100 British people eventually marry.

The famous Treaty of Versailles, signed in 1783, by which Britain recognized the independence of the American colonies, is listed as Foreign Office document No 93/8/2.

Spring normally starts on 21 March and ends on 21 June, while Summer generally begins on 22 June and finishes on 22 September, making each season ninety-three days long.

In Dallas, Texas, the scene of the assassination in 1963 of President John F. Kennedy, there are ninety-three gun shops!

The Statue of Liberty is 93 m (305 ft) high, and has a waist measurement of 10·6 m (35 ft). It stands on Bedloe's Island in New York harbour.

A British parliamentary voting record was achieved at the General Election of October 1951 when over 93 per cent of the electorate of Fermanagh and South Tyrone in Ulster went to the polls and returned an Anti-Partition candidate to Westminster.

The smallest English prison still in use is Kingston in Portsmouth, Hampshire, which has ninety-three cells available.

St James's Park, one of London's most pleasant, covers 93 acres (37·7 hectares). Henry VIII acquired it in 1531 to allow him to hunt near his palace of Whitehall.

Though the symphonies of Franz Joseph Haydn (1732–1809) number 104, those between 9 and 19 are never played today, leaving ninety-three written between 1757 and 1795, available for performance.

There is a difference of 93 miles (150 km) in the length of Australia's two greatest rivers, the Darling (1,702 miles; 2,723 km) and the Murray (1,609 miles; 2,575 km), into which the former empties.

94

A new UK passport containing ninety-four pages and valid for ten years became available from May 1973.

The area of the UK is 94,250 sq miles (244,108 sq km).

Ninety-four per cent of urine consists of water.

A French adult drinks on average 94 litres (165 pt) of wine in a year.

Most of the quality programmes screened on British television are marketed worldwide. For example, the popular Granada series *World in Action* has been seen in ninety-four countries.

The TUC founded in 1868, has a membership of 112 trades unions. They represent 11·9 million working people, or 94 per cent of all the unions in Britain.

Pepi II Neferkare was the fifth king of the sixth Egyptian dynasty (*c* 2345–2181 BC). His reign, plagued by domestic troubles, began when he was six, and reputedly lasted for ninety-four years! His pyramid at Saqqarah, facing Cairo across the Nile, was one of the largest ever built.

There are ninety-four professional orchestras in music-loving West Germany.

The complete works of William Shakespeare (1564–1616) have been translated into ninety-four languages, but surely none can do full justice to the original Elizabethan English.

The annual mortality rate among rats and mice is estimated to be 94 per cent.

95

Meteorites are roughly 95 per cent silica and magnesium oxide.

Lettuce, cucumber, mustard and cress – staples of any salad – have a water content of 95 parts in 100.

Algae, single cells which appear like green scum and grow on stagnant water, are themselves 95 per cent water.

France is divided into twenty-one administrative regions and ninety-five departments. Each department is usually named after the chief river flowing through it, and has its own car and mail registration numbers.

Trinity House administers the ninety-five lighthouses around the coast of England, Wales and the Channel Islands.

Ninety-five per cent of bronze is copper, the remainder of the alloy being 4 per cent tin and 1 per cent zinc.

Shortly before his death from overwork and coffee poisoning, the great French novelist Honoré de Balzac (1799–1850) selected ninety-five of his varied works – among them *Père Goriot* and *Le Cousin Pons* – to represent what he called *La Comédie Humaine*.

Steel is never less than 95 per cent iron.

In the Republic of Ireland 95 per cent of the population are Roman Catholics, while nineteen out of every twenty Swedes are Lutherans.

The ninety-five City of London guilds each have a distinctive dress or livery first adopted in the fourteenth century. The oldest members are the Mercers, the Grocers, the Drapers, the Fishmongers and the Goldsmiths.

96

Ninety-six per cent of the atmosphere of Venus is carbon dioxide.

After thirty-two weeks 96 per cent of unborn babies will assume a head first position ready for birth.

By British law, when a person dies a death certificate must be obtained, and the place and manner of funeral arranged, within ninety-six hours.

Biggles, otherwise known as Squadron-Leader Bigglesworth, ace flyer and daredevil, was featured in ninety-six thrilling adventure tales by the late Captain W. E. Johns.

After ninety-six years the penalty for the improper use of a communication cord in a railway carriage was raised from £5 to £25 on 8 September 1965.

Of the ninety-six kinds of pine trees, all except sixteen are found in the northern hemisphere. Mexico, between latitude 15–30°N of the equator, has the greatest number of varieties.

Ten thousand children auditioned for ninety-six parts in the stage version of Alan Parker's film of New York's gangland, *Bugsy Malone*, which was a box-office hit in 1983.

Goodbye Mr Chips, *Dead of Night* and *Kind Hearts and Coronets* were just three of the ninety-six highly acclaimed films directed by Sir Michael Balcon for Ealing studio productions between 1938 and 1956.

Diogenes, a Greek cynic who lived in a portable tub, died in 323 BC aged ninety-six. His body was returned to his birthplace Sinope on the Black Sea coast, statues were erected in his memory and a symbolic head of a dog – the kind of life he led – surmounted his richly decorated tomb!

According to a recent survey, a vocabulary of only 737 words was used in 96 per cent of all American telephone conversations.

97

American-born Harry Gordon Selfridge placed ninety-seven full-page advertisements in the national daily newspapers during the week preceding the opening in 1909 of his revolutionary department store on Oxford Street, London.

Ninety-seven per cent of French adults have bank accounts compared to only fifty-one per cent of Britons.

The ever busy Queen Mother was eighty-two when she carried out ninety-seven official engagements in 1982, including two to Northern Ireland.

Ninety-seven is the last prime number below a hundred.

Polish vodka and raw rum are best avoided: they are both 97 per cent alcohol. Alcoholics Anonymous, formed to assist those with drink problems, has branches in ninety-seven countries.

The Kent wicket-keeper Godfrey Evans 'batted' for a record ninety-seven minutes without scoring a run in a successful effort to save England from defeat in the fourth Test against Australia at Adelaide on 6 February 1947. Well played, sir!

More than 97 per cent of car engines use the four stroke cycle, the most efficient being the water-cooled four cylinder unit.

Founded by Lt Gen (later Lord) Robert Baden-Powell in 1908 when he was fifty, the Boy Scouts (now the Scout Association) had spread to ninety-seven countries by 1972 (16 million members).

The Liverpool to Manchester Railway – the first for public use in the world – opened its service in 1830 with only 97 miles (156 km) of track.

The fourth Gospel has been ascribed to John, the son of Zebedee, and one of the original twelve disciples. His mother was probably the sister of Mary, the mother of Jesus. He penned his story of the Lord's life when he was ninety-seven and living at Ephesus in Asia Minor.

98

On 26 August 55 BC, Julius Caesar's exploratory expedition to Britain set sail from Ambleteuse and Boulogne. A fleet of ninety-eight ships was required to transport the 7th and 10th legions and their equipment.

By 1855, 98 per cent of all the public clocks in the UK were adjusted to Greenwich Mean Time.

Although one of the world's leading industrialized nations, Japan has to import 98 per cent of its iron ore!

There are ninety-eight muscles in the human arms – ten less than in the lower limbs.

The great Sir John (Jack) Hobbs (1882–1963) – probably the best ever English batsman – hit ninety-eight of his record 197 cricket centuries after his fortieth birthday!

Scotland's two longest rivers, the Clyde and the Spey, are both 98 miles (157·7 km) in length.

By the time they are forty 98 per cent of the women in the western world have bunions.

Ninety-eight people were victims of terrorism in Northern Ireland in 1982.

Denmark graciously granted complete independence to Iceland in June 1944, after 98 per cent of the inhabitants had voted in favour of ending a tie dating back to 1380.

By 1981, 98 per cent of British homes had some kind of television installed.

99

The Germans surrendered on 7 May 1945, and the Japanese (after enduring two atomic bombs) on 14 August – ninety-nine days later. These events concluded World War II.

Property leases in Britain are usually for ninety-nine years.

Only ninety-nine of Denmark's 483 islands are inhabited.

Ninety-nine per cent of all the milk sold in Britain is bottled.

Calcium can be traced in the blood, nerves, teeth and muscles, but 99 per cent of it is residual in the bones.

Between 1965 and 1973 the Scot Jackie Stewart made ninety-nine starts and won a record twenty-seven Grand Prixs. He was World Motor Racing Champion in 1969, 1971 and 1973.

The *Evening News* closed down after ninety-nine years of continuous publication in November 1980, leaving London with only the *Standard* for commuters to read on their way home from work.

In 1953 an estimated 99 per cent of the British rabbit population was exterminated by myxomatosis, a dreadful disease carried and spread by fleas.

The world's quietest room is in the laboratory of the Bell Telephone System at Mercury Hall, New Jersey, USA, where, incredibly, 99·98 per cent of reflected sound has been eliminated.

Of the first 100 people to be awarded the prestigious Order of Merit, ninety-nine were men. The sole woman was Florence Nightingale (1820–1910), the twenty-second recipient in 1907.

100

Shetland ponies when fully grown stand only 100 cm (39 in) high.

On 19 October 1973, Mary Simpson and her brother Robert Bean of Birkenhead, Merseyside, became the first known British twins ever to reach the age of 100.

At Headingley, Leeds, in 1977, Yorkshire's star batsman Geoffrey Boycott scored his 100th century, in the Test match against Australia.

Giovanni Boccaccio (1313–75) was thirty-five when he wrote the *Decameron*, 100 licentious but often very humorous tales conceived to be related by seven ladies and three gentlemen over a period of ten evenings at a country house outside the plague-stricken Italian city of Florence.

In the Bible story David had to kill 100 Philistines, chief enemy of the Israelites, before he was allowed to marry Michal, the youngest daughter of King Saul.

Steam at 100°C (212°F) occupies 1,700 times the volume of water at the same temperature.

In 1935 it was possible to buy for just £100 the latest Ford 8 hp Model Y, better known to motorists as the Popular, and a car which certainly lived up to its name.

A streak of lightning passing from cloud to cloud may measure as much as 100 miles (161 km) in length. A single stroke would provide enough energy to light a 100-watt bulb for three months.

William K. Vanderbilt (1849–1920), a member of one of America's wealthiest families, treated himself to a garage with space to accommodate 100 cars at his mansion on Long Island, New York.

During the first 100 days from the opening of the Colosseum, Rome, in AD 80, more than 5,000 animals were killed. They included elephants, lions, tigers, elks, hyenas, hippopotami and giraffes.